MIRACLE KOREAN

1. Learn to Read and Write Hangul

ORIDORI

The Simplest Way to Learn Hangul

Welcome to Miracle Korean

Congratulations on deciding to learn Korean! With the right approach, Hangul(Hangeul)—the Korean alphabet—is something anyone can master quickly. Created by native Seoul Korean speakers after years of research, *Miracle Korean* makes learning Hangul easy. With our specially designed curriculum, just 10 minutes a day is all it takes. In only 26 days, you'll be reading and writing Hangul with confidence.

Why Our Method Works

How is this possible? *Miracle Korean*'s courses are built on the original principles behind the creation of Hangul. In other words, they stay true to the fundamentals. This simple yet powerful approach is often overlooked by other textbooks, which tend to stick to more conventional methods.

At *Miracle Korean*, we've redesigned our curriculum for maximum efficiency. For example, instead of following the traditional order, letters are grouped by visual similarity—making them easier to recognize and remember. We've also streamlined the most challenging parts of Hangul, like vowel combinations and double final consonants, and made sound change rules simple to understand.

Focused on What Really Matters

Let's be honest—more pages don't always mean better learning. What really matters is having only the essential information. That's why we focused on what actually helps you learn faster and smarter, cutting out everything you don't need. This is what sets *Miracle Korean* apart.

Every part of this book is designed for maximum clarity and efficiency. With the textbook, workbook, and video lectures all included, you'll have everything you need right here—no extra materials required.

Just 10 Minutes a Day: Your Journey Starts Now!

Learning doesn't have to be time-consuming. All you need is the right curriculum. If you believe in smart, efficient learning— the core of our philosophy—you're already on the right path to real progress. Just 10 minutes a day is all it takes. Start learning Korean today—it's your key to new opportunities!

함께 시작해요!

Table of
CONTENTS

Chapter 01

음절구조

SYLLABLE STRUCTURE

DAY 01 Syllable Structure

Sejong the Great and the Creation of Hangul

Back in 1443, King Sejong the Great created Hunmin-jeongeum—what we now call Hangul. His goal was simple but powerful: to give everyone in Joseon an easier way to read and write. At that time, people had to use complicated Chinese characters, which were difficult to learn. Hangul changed that. It was designed so ordinary people could quickly pick it up, opening the door to education and communication for all. This vision has been carried forward through the centuries, and Hangul is still at the heart of Korean literacy and culture today.

Definition of a Syllable: The Sound Block of Hangul

One of the fundamental concepts for understanding Hangul is the structure of syllables. Think of them as little boxes that hold sounds. In Korean, letters fit together inside these boxes to form syllables, and syllables then join up to create words.

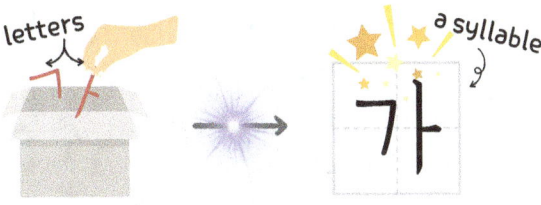

letters

a syllable

Joseon (조선) is a Korean dynastic kingdom that lasted for 505 years, until the Korean Empire replaced it in October 1897.

A syllable can also be described as a unit of sound. For example, in English, the word **bat** has just one syllable: **bat**. But the word **banana** has three: **ba—na—na**. Each syllable is made by arranging letters in a certain pattern. In Hangul, this pattern is fixed, with clear spots for consonants and vowels inside the syllable box.

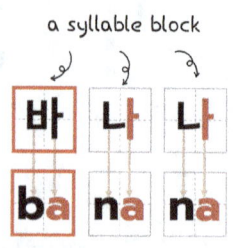

a syllable block

The positions of the consonants and vowels cannot be switched.

Syllable Components: Vowels and Consonants

These positions, which are not random but follow a standardized structure, vary depending on the combination of vowels and consonants within a syllable unit.

Vowels* are sounds made with an open vocal tract. In other words, the tongue and lips don't touch anything in the mouth. Because of this openness, vowels can be pronounced on their own. But when paired with consonants, they form complete syllables. Consonants, on the other hand, involve some kind of contact—such as in the sounds **b**, **t**, or **s**. That's what gives them a clear, defined sound.

One key difference between vowels and consonants in Hangul is the number of sounds each letter can represent. <u>A vowel always keeps the same sound. A consonant, however, can change depending on its position within the syllable</u>: it has one sound when it comes at the start of a syllable (initial consonant), and another when it comes at the end of a syllable (final consonant).

Vowels in English consist of the letters a, e, i, o, and u.

Every Hangul syllable needs at least one consonant and one vowel to make a sound. On top of that, an extra consonant—called the **받침** (batchim, or final consonant)—can be added at the bottom of the syllable block. It's important to remember the batchim, because <u>whether it's there or not can change how grammar works in Korean</u>.

To recap, each syllable, or sound block, consists of the following components:

- Initial position(sound): a consonant (**자음**)
- Medial position(sound): a vowel (**모음**)

} The basic building blocks of a syllable

- Final position(sound): a consonant (=a batchim, **받침**)

HANGUL HACK

What does '받침 *Batchim*' mean?

Q) What do the circled items have in common?

In Korean, the word **받침** refers to 'something placed underneath to provide support.' For example, a coaster(**컵받침**) is called a cup(**컵**) batchim(**받침**), and a pot stand(**화분받침**) is called a hwabun(**화분**, pot) batchim(**받침**). <u>The final consonant in a syllable block is called</u> **batchim** <u>because it 'supports' the arrangement of consonants and vowels within the block.</u>

A) All of them are <u>BATCHIMs</u>!

Order of Reading and Writing:

Consonant → Vowel → (Final Consonant, if there is one)

A Hangul syllable—also called a sound block—can have up to three parts: the initial consonant (초성), the vowel (중성), and the final consonant (종성), also known as the batchim. These parts are always written and read in the same order: ① initial consonant → ② vowel → ③ final consonant (if there is one).

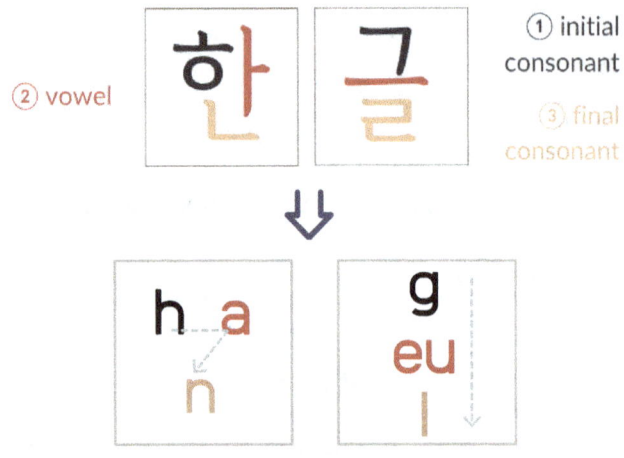

The colored letters match the sounds of the Korean letters in the same color.

In the illustration above, the sequence from ① to ③ shows this fixed order. Simply follow the arrows in the illustration below to read the sounds in the correct sequence. One key point to remember: the vowel is always in the second position—either next to or under the initial consonant. Whether it goes next to or beneath depends on the vowel's shape, which we'll explain in more detail later.

DAY 02 Letter Arrangement

Letter Placement Within a Syllable

The way letters are arranged inside a syllable depends on two things: how many parts the syllable has and the shape of the vowel. Below is a simple overview of the main patterns you'll see.

A. Two—letter syllable (CV): Consonant + Vowel

This is the basic structure of a Korean syllable, consisting of one consonant and one vowel. The way the consonant and vowel are placed inside a syllable block changes depending on the vowel's shape:

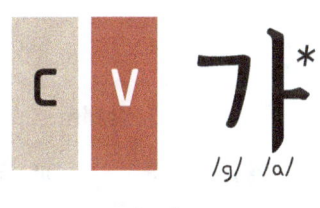

/ga/

A—1. When the vowel has a vertical shape:
- Vertical vowels: ㅏ, ㅑ, ㅓ, ㅕ, ㅣ, ㅐ, ㅒ, ㅖ, ㅐ ㅒ
- The consonant is placed to the left of the syllable's central axis.
- The vowel is positioned to the right.

/go/

A—2. When the vowel has a horizontal shape:
- Horizontal vowels: ㅗ, ㅛ, ㅜ, ㅠ, ㅡ
- The consonant is placed at the top of the syllable block, above the midpoint of its horizontal axis.
- The vowel is positioned below the consonant.

*ㄱ *makes the /g/ or /k/ sound.* ㅏ *makes the /a/ sound.*

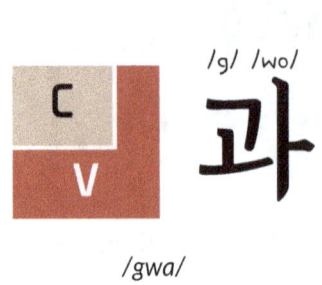

/g/ /wo/

과

/gwa/

A—3. When the vowel has a complex shape (combination of vertical and horizontal vowels)

- Complex vowels: ㅘ,ㅚ,ㅝ, and so on
- The consonant is placed in the upper—left corner of the syllable block.
- The vowel is positioned in the right and lower parts of the syllable block.

B. Three—letter syllable (CVC): Consonant + Vowel + Batchim

When there's a batchim (final consonant), it goes underneath the main vowel shape(CV). To write it, imagine the syllable block split into two parts: the top for the vowel shape, and the bottom for the final consonant. Make sure to write the batchim neatly in its spot at the bottom.

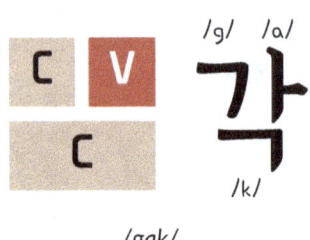

/g/ /a/

각

/k/

/gak/

B—1. A1 (C.+Vertial V.) + Batchim

- The initial consonant is set to the left of the syllable's central axis.
- The vowel is placed to the right.
- The batchim positioned at the bottom.

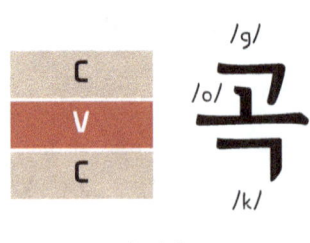

/g/

/o/

곡

/k/

/gok/

B—2. A2 (C. + Horizontal V.) + Batchim

- The initial consonant is placed at the top of the syllable block.
- The vowel is positioned below the consonant.
- The batchim is located at the bottom.

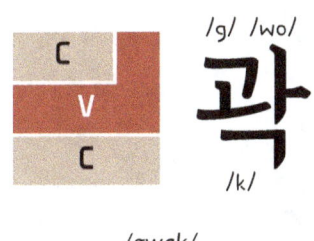

/g/ /wo/

곽

/k/

/gwak/

B—3. A3 (C.+ Complex V.) + Batchim

•The initial consonant is placed to the left of the syllable's central axis.

•The vertical part of the vowel is placed to the right of the initial consonant, while the horizontal part is positioned beneath the initial consonant.

•The batchim positioned at the bottom.

C. Syllables with double consonants: Arrange them like a single consonants

Sometimes you'll see more complex Hangul syllables with double consonants, like ㄲ, ㄸ, or ㅃ, or double final consonants, like ㄶ, ㄼ, or ㅄ. At first, these syllables may look like they follow complicated patterns, such as CCVC or CCVCC.

But don't worry—they still fit into the **A**(CV) and **B**(CVC) structures we covered earlier. The key is to treat each double consonant as just one unit when you place it in the syllable.

For example, in the picture below, ㄲ isn't two separate ㄱs. It acts as a single consonant and goes into the consonant slot of the syllable block, just like any other single consonant.

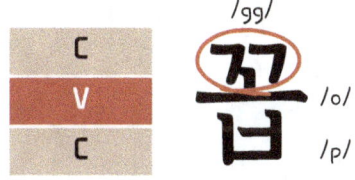

/gg/

꼽

/o/

/p/

/ggop/

A double consonant is still placed in the consonant position.

Likewise, ㅄ is not made up of ㅂ and ㅅ as individual letters. Within a syllable, ㅄ is placed in the consonant position.

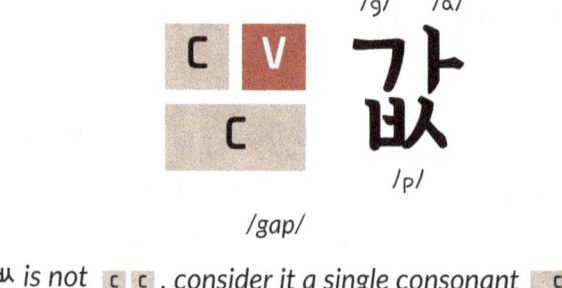

/gap/

ㅄ *is not* ㄷ ㄷ *, consider it a single consonant* ㄷ

To start reading and writing Hangul effectively, we'll follow this order: basic vowels → basic consonants → double vowels → double consonants. This sequence works well because most Korean words can already be read with just the basic vowels and consonants. Double letters, on the other hand, often come with exceptions, so it's easier to learn them later—after you've built a solid foundation with the basics.

DAY 03 Sound Changes in ㅇ

ㅇ as a _Silent Placeholder_ at the Beginning of a Syllable (Initial Consonant)

Previously, we learned that <u>every syllable requires at least one consonant and one vowel</u>. However, the <u>initial and final consonants are not always necessary</u>. Doesn't this seem contradictory? If a syllable must include at least one consonant, how can some syllables have none at all? How can both statements be true?

When there is no final consonant, it's simple. You just end the syllable with the second sound, which is the vowel. However, in cases where there is no initial consonant, the consonant **ㅇ** _(ieung)_ acts as a placeholder. This is because, in Korean, every syllable must begin with a consonant, even if it's silent. For example, in the syllable **아**, the silent **ㅇ** occupies the consonant position, allowing the vowel to produce the syllable's only sound.

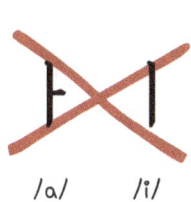

/a/   /i/

silent ㅇ

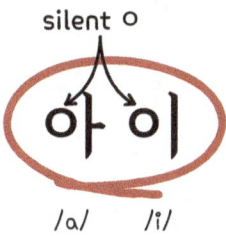

/a/   /i/

In Miracle Korean, we learn vowels before consonants. That's why you will often encounter syllables with the silent consonant **ㅇ** in the vowel section. In these cases, **ㅇ** does not produce a sound, and you only pronounce the vowel in the syllable.

In contrast, when ㅇ is used as a final consonant, it makes the **/ng/** sound, as in **Wing** or **Sing**. As shown in the examples below, adding the final consonant ㅇ to a base syllable changes both the pronunciation and the meaning of the word.

자 /ja/ ruler   조 /jo/ trillion   차 /cha/ car   초 /cho/ candle

+ㅇ

장 /jang/ page, chapter   종 /jong/ bell   창 /chang/ window   총 /chong/ gun

How to Write Hangul Neatly

What Makes Hangul Look So Neat and Organized?

There is a story—though unproven to be true—that suggests King Sejong designed Hangul by observing window and door frames. While this may not be true, it provides a possible explanation for why printed Hangul looks so neat and precise, like a well—organized bookshelf. Handwriting, though, can be a different story: keeping those tidy blocks on paper takes practice. Build good habits early and you'll save time and effort later. Here are some tips to help you write Korean neatly from the start.

A. Understanding the Syllable Structure

A Hangul syllable has a fixed layout with set slots for each letter, as we discussed earlier. Spend a little time getting comfortable with these base patterns. When you know where each part goes, your hand knows what to write next—so you can write more smoothly and confidently.

B. Keeping Your Syllable Blocks Consistent in Size

To make your writing neat and easy to read, try to keep your syllable blocks roughly the same size. Grid paper can be a helpful tool to guide you and ensure each block stays tidy and uniform.

In neat writing, syllables are uniform in size.
Consonants and vowels are well–balanced within each syllable.

C. Making Strokes Parallel at a Steady Angle

Hangul letters are built from simple shapes: straight lines, circles, and short strokes. The shapes themselves are easy, but a few techniques can help you write them more neatly and precisely.

Try to keep your strokes even in length and angle. This makes each syllable look more balanced and visually pleasing. Also, keep parallel strokes at a steady angle—this small habit goes a long way in making your handwriting clear and tidy. Now, compare the handwriting in examples 1 and 2. Which one looks neater and more polished to you?

① 안 녕   안 녕

② 안녕   안 녕

Most people would likely prefer example 2 because its balanced vertical and horizontal lines give it a more polished appearance.

The vertical and horizontal lines are NOT parallel to each other.

The vertical and horizontal lines are parallel to each other.

Keep this tip in mind as you practice writing Hangul. This will help your handwriting become more precise and neat!

Chapter 02

기본모음

BASIC VOWELS

DAY 04 Basic Vowels

Consistency in Vowel Sounds

IIn Hangul, vowels are based on three symbolic elements: a dot or short line representing the sky, a horizontal line symbolizing the Earth, and a vertical line representing man.

Chun 天
sky, heaven

Ji 地
Earth

In 人
man

One unique feature of Hangul vowels is that each one always makes a single, consistent sound. For example, the vowel ㅏ is always pronounced /a/. This is very different from English, where one letter, like **A**, can have several sounds—/æ/, /ɑ/, or /ə/, depending on the word.

As shown below, the vowel sound in Hangul stays the same. What changes is the initial consonant that comes before it. For instance, the syllable 아 is pronounced only as /a/, since the ㅇ is a silent placeholder (as we learned back in Chapter 1).

ㄱㅏ → 가	ㄴㅏ → 나
/g/ /a/ /ga/	/g/ /a/ /na/
ㄷㅏ → 다	ㄹㅏ → 라
/d/ /a/ /da/	/l/ /a/ /la/
ㅁㅏ → 마	ㅇㅏ → 아
/m/ /a/ /ma/	silent /a/ /a/

Linguistic Classification of Hangul Vowels: Monophthongs and Diphthongs

In Korean linguistics, Hangul vowels are classified into 10 monophthongs and 11 diphthongs. The difference comes from whether the tongue and mouth stay in one shape or shift during pronunciation.

- Monophthongs: These are pure, simple vowel sounds. The tongue and mouth remain steady without shifting during pronunciation.

- Diphthongs: These are more dynamic, involving a smooth transition between two sounds within a single syllable. Often, they combine a main vowel with a semivowel or another vowel, creating a flowing "sliding" sound.

The table below gives you a quick overview of the vowel types.

Linguistic Classification of Vowels

Feature	Monophthongs	Diphthongs
Sound Quality	Single, pure sound	Gliding, combined sound
Tongue Movement	No change	Moves between positions
Examples in Hangul	ㅏ, ㅐ, ㅓ, ㅔ, ㅗ, ㅚ, ㅜ, ㅟ, ㅡ, ㅣ	ㅒ, ㅖ, ㅙ, ㅞ, ㅑ, ㅕ, ㅛ, ㅠ, ㅘ, ㅝ, ㅢ

Linguistic classifications can be interesting, but they don't usually come up in everyday conversations. If you're studying for a Korean exam, it's worth reviewing this section. Otherwise, feel free to skip it for now—you won't miss anything important in daily use.

Miracle Korean's Intuitive Classification of Vowels by Shape

Oridori's *Miracle Korean* is designed to help non-native speakers learn practical Korean quickly and effectively. To make things easier, this book groups vowels by their shapes and sounds, using a simple and intuitive system—different from the linguistic classification on the previous page. In this system, the 21 Korean vowels are divided into two groups: 10 basic vowels and 11 double vowels. In this chapter, we'll start with the basic vowels.

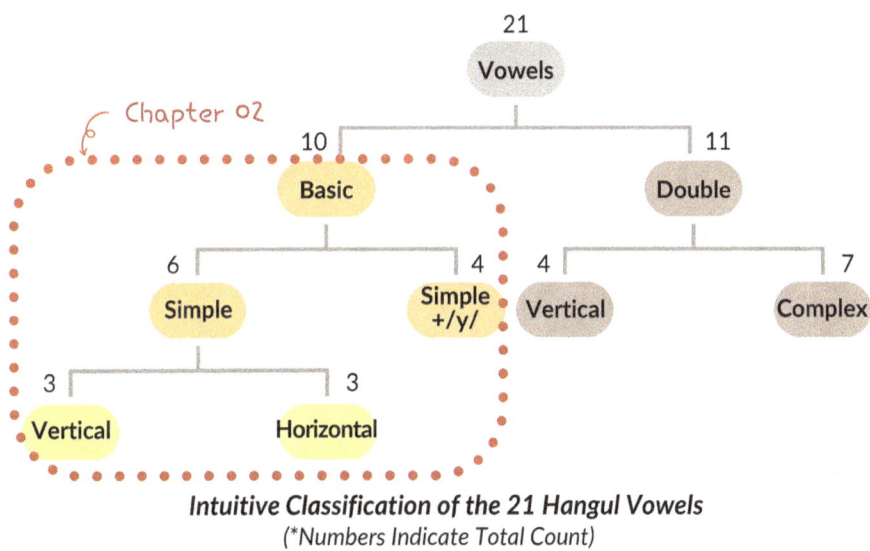

Intuitive Classification of the 21 Hangul Vowels
(*Numbers Indicate Total Count)

Basic vowels make one clear sound without blending. Compound vowels, on the other hand, are created by joining two basic vowels into a single sound. The 10 basic vowels can be grouped into two categories:

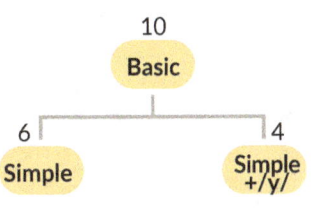

- Simple vowels: ㅏ, ㅓ, ㅗ, ㅜ, ㅡ, and ㅣ. Made up of either <u>a single long stroke</u> or <u>a long stroke paired with a shorter one</u>.
- Simple /y/ vowels: ㅑ, ㅕ, ㅛ, and ㅠ. Made up of <u>a long stroke AND two shorter strokes.</u>

The table below shows all 10 basic vowels. The Romanized notation follow the official system set by the *National Institute of Korean Language*. But remember—Romanized notation is only a tool to show sounds with letters, and it doesn't perfectly match real Korean pronunciation. That's why it's so important to listen to native Korean audio and practice making the sounds yourself.

10 Basic Vowels

	Category	Letter	Pronunciation	Shape
10 Basic Vowels	Simple	ㅏ	/a/	Vertical
		ㅓ	/eo/	Vertical
		ㅗ	/o/	Horizontal
		ㅜ	/u/	Horizontal
		ㅡ	/eu/	Horizontal
		ㅣ	/i/, /ee/	Vertical
	Simple +/y(ㅡ)/	ㅑ	/ya/	Vertical (ㅏ+ㅡ)
		ㅕ	/yeo/	Vertical (ㅓ+ㅡ)
		ㅛ	/yo/	Horizontal (ㅛ+ㅡ)
		ㅠ	/yu/	Horizontal (ㅜ+ㅡ)

25

Roman–letter Notation of the National Language (Official guideline)

Hangul		ㄱ	ㄲ	ㄴ	ㄷ	ㄸ	ㄹ	ㅁ	ㅂ	ㅃ	ㅅ	ㅆ	ㅇ	ㅈ	ㅉ	ㅊ	ㅋ	ㅌ	ㅍ	ㅎ
Romanization	Initial	g	kk	n	d	tt	r	m	b	pp	s	ss	–	j	jj	ch	k	t	p	h
	Final	k	k	n	t	–	l	m	p	–	t	t	ng	t	–	t	k	t	p	t

Hangul	ㅏ	ㅐ	ㅑ	ㅒ	ㅓ	ㅔ	ㅕ	ㅖ	ㅗ	ㅘ	ㅙ	ㅚ	ㅛ	ㅜ	ㅝ	ㅞ	ㅟ	ㅠ	ㅡ	ㅢ	ㅣ
Romanization	a	ae	ya	yae	eo	e	yeo	ye	o	wa	wae	oe	yo	u	wo	we	wi	yu	eu	ui	i

Source: National Institute of Korean Language

DAY 05

ㅏ and ㅓ

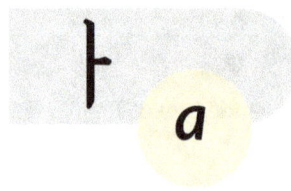
a

The Korean vowel ㅏ sounds similar to the /a/ in English words like **C_ar_** or **F_a_ther**. It's a short, open vowel sound, easy to pronounce and and very common in Korean.

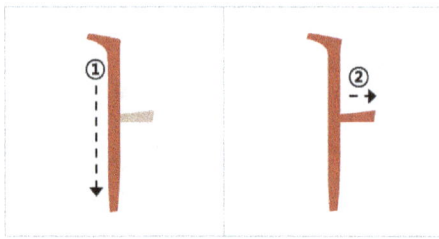

To write ㅏ, first draw a straight line from top to bottom. Then, add a short line on the right side.

🖎 Trace the syllable 아 and get used to where the consonant ㅇ (the silent placeholder) sits in the block.

Say the word out loud and trace the ㅏ in the block.

Silent Placeholder
(no sound)

아 아
/a a/
the abbreviated slang for
'Iced Americano'

아 시 아
/s/ /i/
/a—si—a/
Asia

아 가
/g/
/a—ga/
baby

아 이
/i/
/a—i/
kid

아 마
/m/
/a—ma/
probably, perhaps, maybe

아 파 트
/t/
/p/ /eu/
/a—pa—teu/
apartment

28

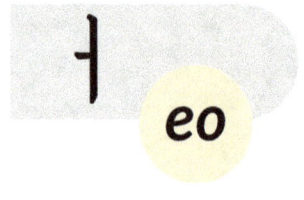

The sound of ㅓ is similar to the *u* sound in *S<u>u</u>n* or the *o* sound in *D<u>o</u>ne*. It's a short, mid-open vowel sound. To make it, place your tongue just a little lower than the neutral position.

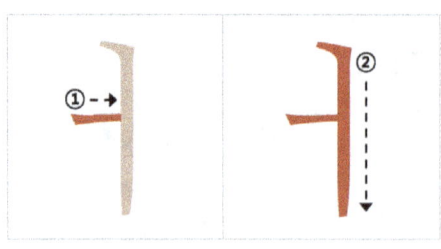

To write ㅓ, first draw a short horizontal line. Then, add a straight vertical line from top to bottom on the right side.

✏ Trace the syllable 어 and get used to how the consonant ㅇ sits inside the block.

어 어 어 어

 Say the word out loud and trace the ㅓ in the block.

. ㄴ : /n/
. ㅡ : /eu/

어 ㄴ

/eo—neu/
which

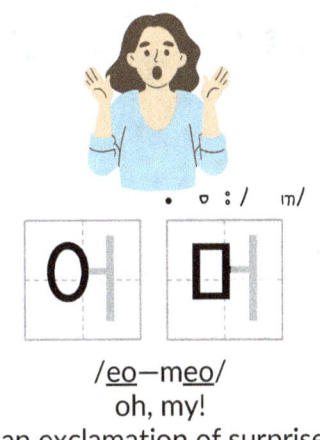

. ㅁ : / m/

어 머

/eo—meo/
oh, my!
;an exclamation of surprise

어 머 니

/eo—meo—ni/
mother

어 부

/eo—bu/
fisherman

어 미

/eo—mi/
female parent
(used for animals)

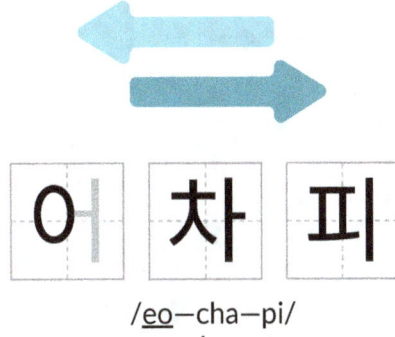

어 차 피

/eo—cha—pi/
anyway, in any case
(Either way, it doesn't matter.)

DAY
06
ㅗ and ㅜ

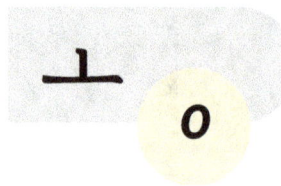

O

The sound of ㅗ in Korean is similar to the **o** sound in G<u>o</u> or B<u>oa</u>t. It's a rounded vowel sound.

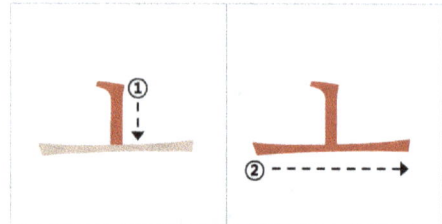

To write ㅗ, draw a short horizontal line. Then, add a straight vertical line from top to bottom on the right side.

✏️ Trace the syllable 오 and get used to where the consonant ㅇ sits in the block.

Say the word out loud and trace the ㅗ in the block.

오 리 /r/ /i/
/o–ri/
duck

오 빠 /pp/
/o–ppa/
older brother, male friend
(used by females)

오 이 /i/
/o–i/
cucumber

오 후 /h/ /u/
/o–hu/
afternoon

오 미 자 /m/ /i/ /j/
/o–mi–ja/
schisandra
(a type of fruit used in
traditional Korean medicine and teas)

오 차 /ch/
/o–cha/
error, deviation

The sound of ㅜ is similar to the /oo(u:)/ sound in M<u>oo</u>n or F<u>oo</u>d. It's a long, rounded vowel sound.

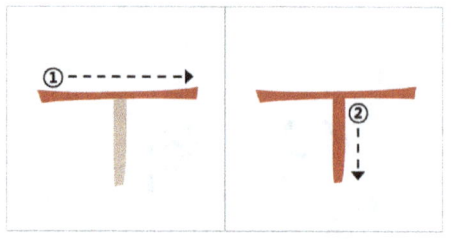

To write ㅜ, draw a long horizontal line. Then, starting from the center of that line, add a short vertical line going down.

✏ Trace the syllable 우 and get used to where the consonant ㅇ sits in the block.

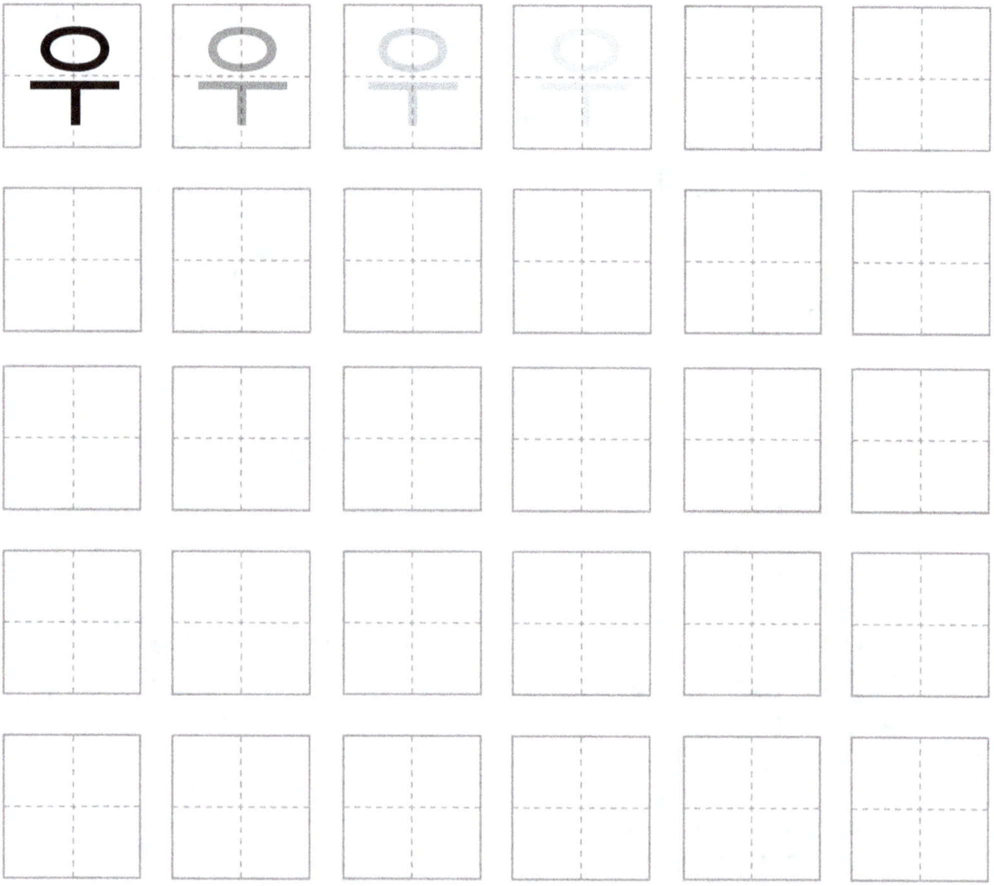

Say the word out loud and trace the ㅜ in the block.

우 기
/g/ /i/

/u‒gi/
rainy season

우 리
/r/ /i/

/u‒ri/
we, us

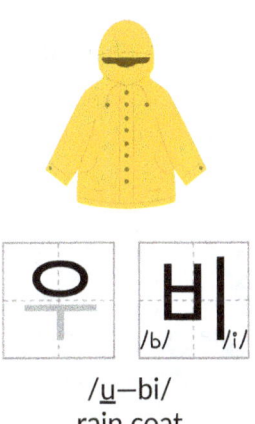

우 비
/b/ /i/

/u‒bi/
rain coat

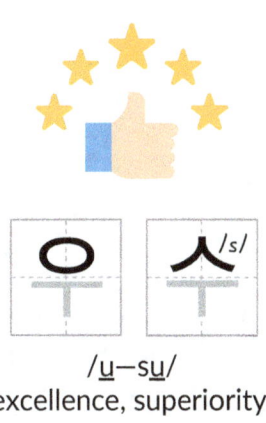

우 스
/s/

/u‒su/
excellence, superiority

우 유
/yu/

/u‒yu/
milk

우 주
/j/

/u‒ju/
space, universe

DAY 07 — and |

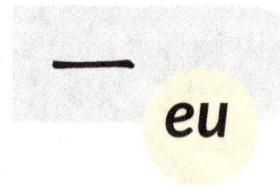
eu

The vowel — doesn't have a perfect match in English, but it's close to the short, flat /oo/ sound in **good**. Try saying the word **good** but keep your lips more relaxed and flat.

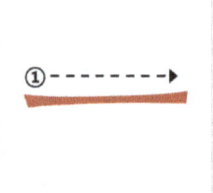

— is very simple to write— just a straight horizontal line.

Trace the syllable 으 and get used to where the consonant ㅇ sits in the block.

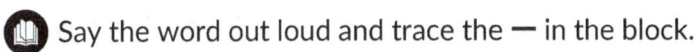 Say the word out loud and trace the ─ in the block.

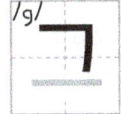

/geu/
that (a specific person or thing
observed by the speaker)

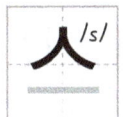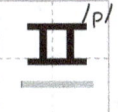

/seu─peu/
soup
(스프 refers to Western─style soups)

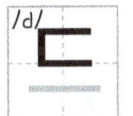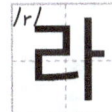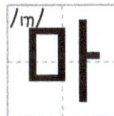

/deu─ra─ma/
TV series

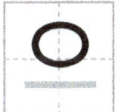

/eu─seu─seu/
creepy or chillily

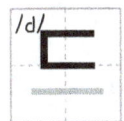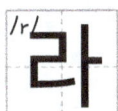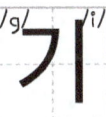

/deu─ra─i─gi/
hair dryer

The sound of ㅣ is like the */i/* sound in the English word *See* or *Tree*. It is like a long, straight */ee/* sound.

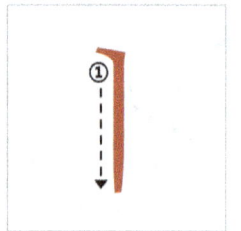

ㅣ is very simple to write— just a straight vertical line.

Trace the syllable 이 and get used to where the consonant ㅇ sits in the block.

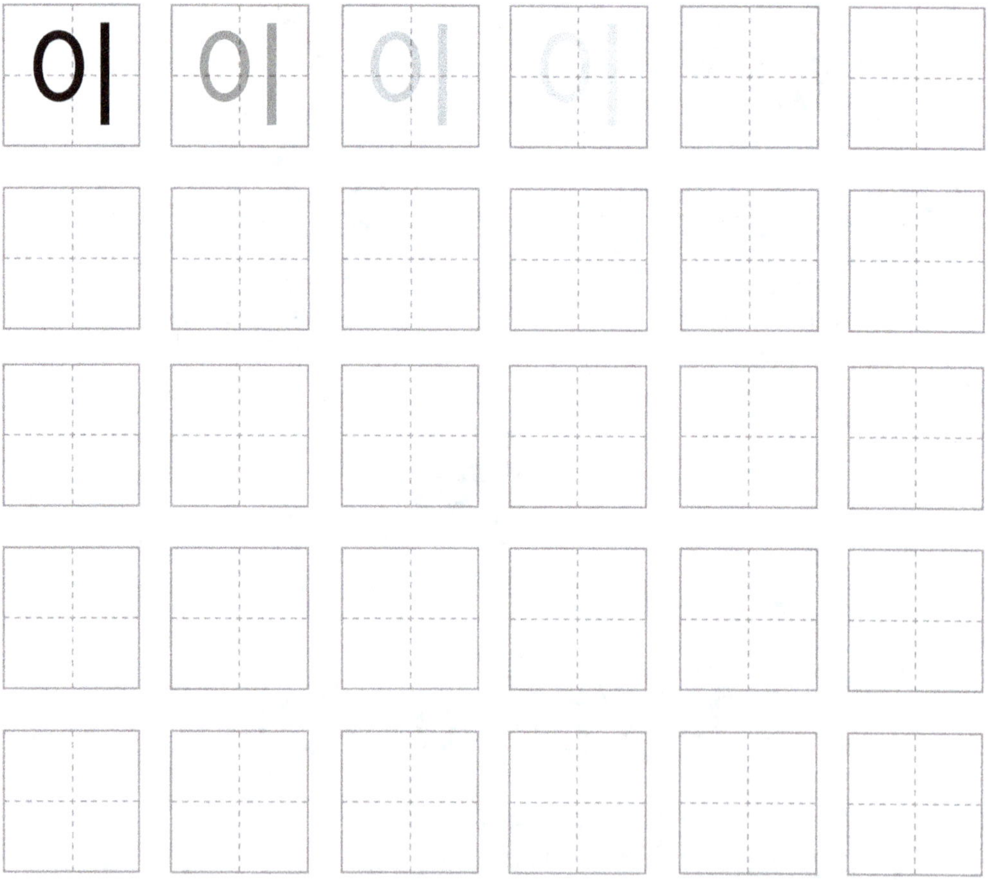

이 이 이 이

Say the word out loud and trace the ㅣ in the block.

이

/i̱/
tooth

이 모 /m/

/i̱—mo/
mother's sister

이 마 /m/

/i̱—ma/
forehead

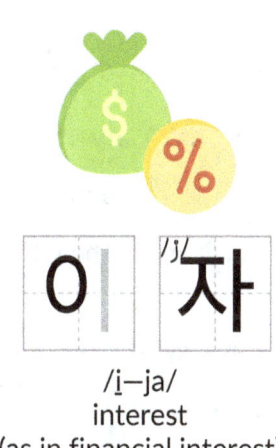

이 자 /j/

/i̱—ja/
interest
(as in financial interest)

이 사 /s/

/i̱—sa/
moving

이 기 /g/ 다 /d/

/i̱—gi̱—da/
to win, the act of winning

DAY 08

ㅑ and ㅕ

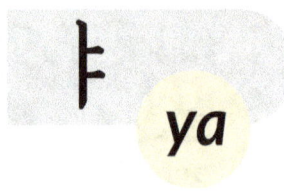

The sound of ㅑ in Korean is similar to the /ya/ sound in the **_Yacht_** or **_Yard_**. It is a combination of the /y/ and /a/ sound.

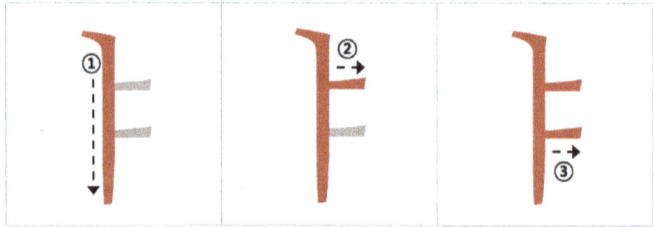

To write ㅑ, draw a vertical line, then add two short horizontal lines on the right. Place the two short lines to divide the long vertical line into three equal parts. This will make the letter look clean and balanced.

✏ Trace the syllable 야 and get used to where the consonant ㅇ sits in the block.

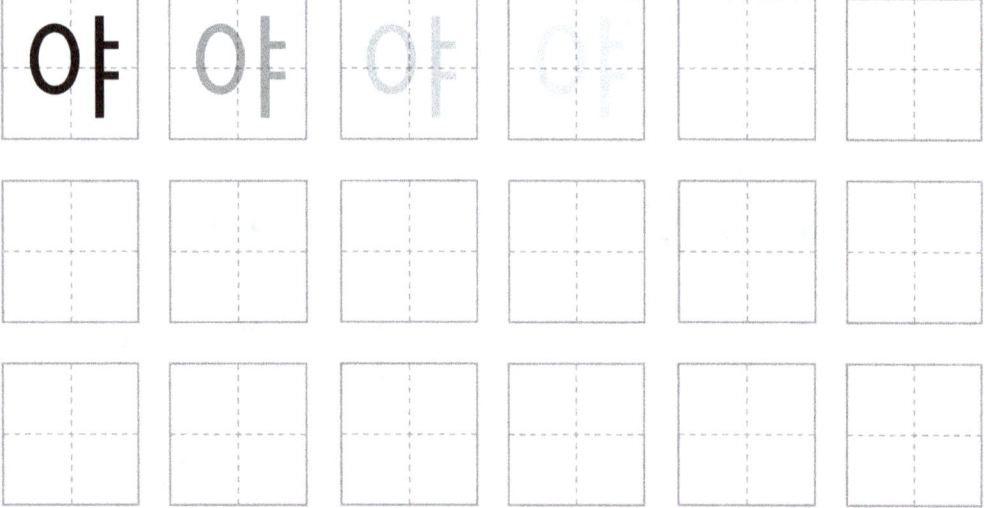

Say the word out loud and trace the ㅑ in the block.

/ya/
hey, you
(a casual way to call a friend
or someone younger than you.)

야 구 /g/

/ya-gu/
baseball

야 수 /s/

/ya-su/
beast

야 유 /yu/

/ya-yu/
jeering, booing, ridiculing

야 자 /j/

/ya-ja/
palm

야 호

/ya-ho/
hooray, yay

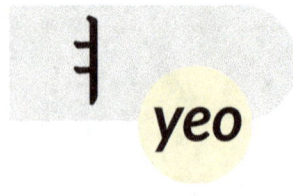

yeo

The sound of ㅕ is similar to the /yo/ sound in **Young**, but it is slightly more open and rounded. It sounds like /yuh/ as in the beginning of **Yum**. It starts with a soft /y/ sound followed by an open, short /uh/ sound.

To write ㅕ, draw two short horizontal lines. Then, add a vertical line on the right side. Just like with ㅑ, ㅕ looks neat and balanced when the two short lines divide the vertical line into three equal parts.

✏ Trace the syllable 여 and get used to where the consonant ㅇ sits in the block.

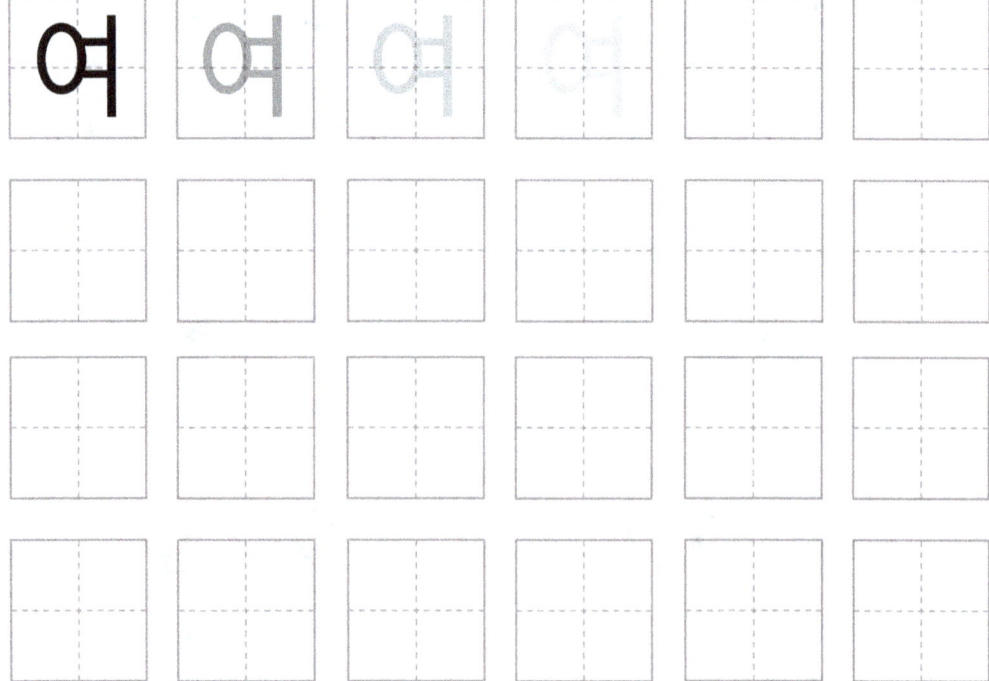

Say the word out loud and trace the ㅕ in the block.

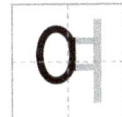 /g/ 가

/yeo–ga/
leisure, free time

 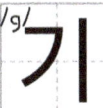 /g/ 기

/yeo–gi/
here

어 우

/yeo–u/
fox

어 유 /yu/

/yeo–yu/
space, room

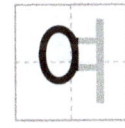  /s/ 사

/yeo–sa/
madam, ma'am

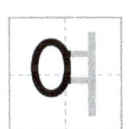 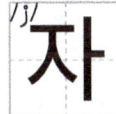 /j/ 자

/yeo–ja/
woman, female

42

DAY 09

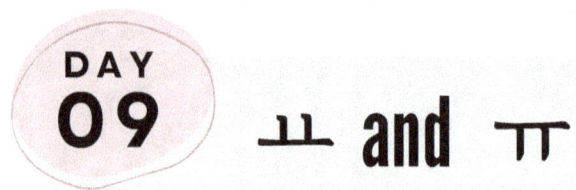

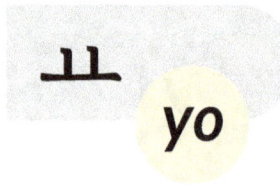

The sound of ㅛ in Korean is similar to the /yo/ sound in *Yoga* or *Yogurt*. But it is shorter sound.

To write ㅛ, first draw two short vertical lines. Then, add one long horizontal line beneath them. Just like with ㅑ or ㅕ, the letter looks neat and balanced when the two short lines divide the horizontal line into three equal parts.

✏️ Trace the syllable 요 and get used to where the consonant ㅇ sits in the block.

43

Say the word out loud and trace the ㅛ in the block.

요 가 /g/

/yo–ga/
yoga

요 구 /g/

/yo–gu/
request

요 소 /s/

/yo–so/
component, factor

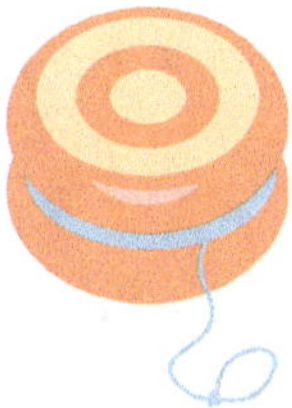

요 요

/yo–yo/
yo–yo

요 리 /r/

/yo–ri/
cooking

요 트 /t/

/yo–teu/
yacht

44

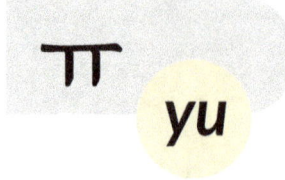

The sound of ㅠ is similar to the */you/* sound in **You** or */u/* sound in **Use**. However, it is pronounced with more rounded lips and a higher tongue position.

To write ㅠ, draw a long horizontal line. Then, add two short vertical lines beneath it. Just like with ㅛ, the letter looks neat and balanced when the two short strokes divide the horizontal line into three equal parts.

✎ Trace the syllable 유 and get used to where the consonant ㅇ sits in the block.

 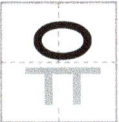

/u–yu/
milk

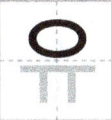 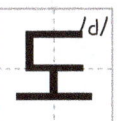

/yu–do/
Judo
(a type of sports)

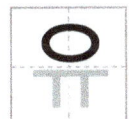 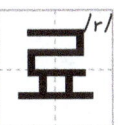

/yu–ryo/
paid, not for free

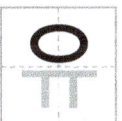 

/yu–ri/
glass

/yu–a/
infant, toddler

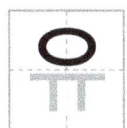 

/yu–ja/
yuzu

Practice writing Hangul in any way you like!

Chapter 03

기본자음
BASIC CONSONANTS

DAY 10

Basic Consonants

Getting to Know Consonant Sounds

As we mentioned earlier, the pronunciation of a consonant changes depending on its position in a syllable block. Unlike vowels, which keep consistent and steady sounds, consonants can shift depending on whether they come at the beginning of a syllable or in the batchim (final) position. Out of the 30 consonants in Hangul, only seven (ㄱ, ㄴ, ㄷ, ㄹ, ㅁ, ㅂ, and ㅇ) are used as valid final sounds. Because of this, different consonants may sound identical when placed in the batchim position.

19 Basic Consonants: Function as Either Initial or Batchim

Korean has 19 basic consonants, divided into three categories: 10 simple consonants, 4 aspirated consonants, and 5 tense consonants. These consonants can be used at both the beginning (initial consonant) and the end (batchim) of a syllable.

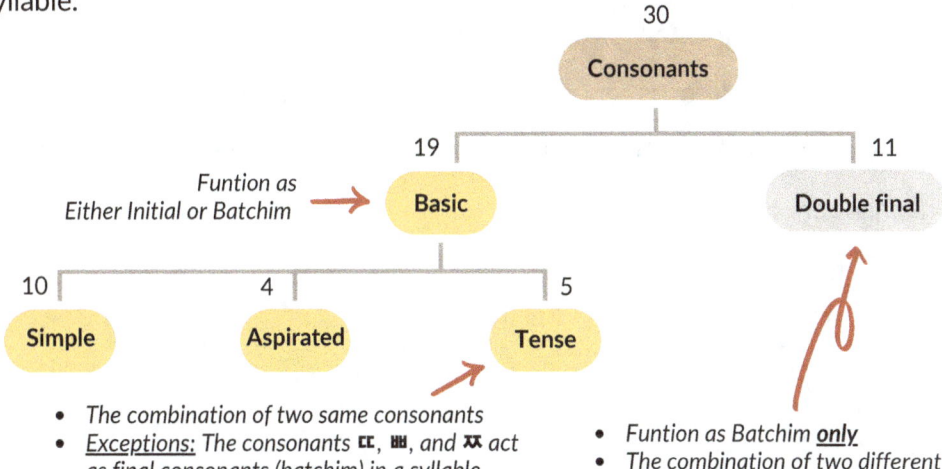

- The combination of two same consonants
- _Exceptions:_ The consonants ㄸ, ㅃ, and ㅉ act as final consonants (batchim) in a syllable.

- Funtion as Batchim _only_
- The combination of two different consonants

SSimple consonants form the base of Korean pronunciation. They represent the basic tongue movements inside the mouth. Some of these consonants also have aspirated or tense versions, which require extra force and control. For beginners, these can feel tricky to tell apart because both are pronounced quickly and with strong articulation. <u>The main difference is this: aspirated sounds come with a burst of air, while tense sounds do not.</u>

HANGUL HACK   **Helpful tip to distinguish between ㅋ and ㄲ**

Hold a tissue in front of your mouth as you pronounce the consonant. If it's aspirated, like ㅋ, the tissue will flutter due to the burst of air. If it's tense, like ㄲ, the tissue will remain still because no air is released. Try this method for practice!

- Tissue moves: Aspirated sound
- Tissue does <u>not</u> move: Tense sound

In this chapter, we'll focus on the 19 basic consonants. To make them easier to grasp, we'll group them by similar shapes instead of following the traditional consonant order*.

*Traditional consonant order: ㄱ,ㄴ,ㄷ,ㄹ,ㅁ,ㅂ,ㅅ,ㅇ,ㅈ,ㅊ,ㅍ,ㅎ

	Letter	Initial	Batchim	Classification
19 Basic Consonants	ㄱ	/g/		simple
	ㅋ	/k/	/k/	aspirated
	ㄲ	/gg/		tense
	ㄷ	/d/		simple
	ㅌ	/t/		aspirated
	ㄸ	/dd/		tense
	ㅈ	/j/	/t/	simple
	ㅊ	/ch/		aspirated
	ㅉ	/jj/		tense
	ㅅ	/s/		simple
	ㅆ	/ss/		tense
	ㅂ	/b/	/p/	simple
	ㅍ	/p/		aspirated

(Following the table on the previous page)

	Letter	Initial	Batchim	Classification
19 Basic Consonants	ㅃ	/bb/	/p/	tense
	ㅇ	silent	/ng/	simple
	ㅎ	/h/	/t/	simple
	ㄴ	/n/	/n/	simple
	ㄹ	/r/	/l/	simple
	ㅁ	/m/	/m/	simple

DAY 11

ㄱ / ㅋ / ㄲ

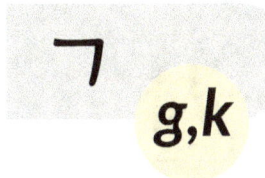

ㄱ
g,k

The sound of **ㄱ**(*Giyeok*,**기역**) changes depending on its position within a syllable. When it comes before a vowel, it is pronounced as /*g*/, as in <u>G</u>o. However, when it appears in the final position after a vowel, it is pronounced as /*k*/, as in Ba<u>k</u>.

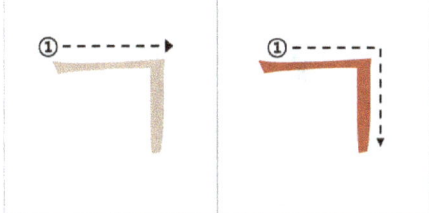

To write **ㄱ**, draw a horizontal line. Without lifting your pencil, draw a vertical line down from the right end.

✏️ Trace each letter and see how **ㄱ** changes its shape with different vowels.

Say the word out loud and trace the ㄱ in the block.

가 구

/ga–gu/
furniture

가 사 /s/

/ga–sa/
lyrics

가 수 /s/

/ga–su/
singer

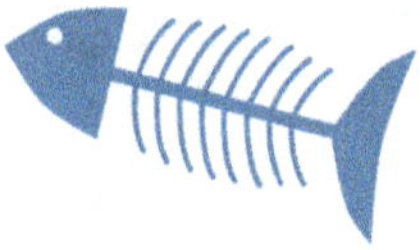

가 시 /s/

/ga–si/
thorn, fishbone

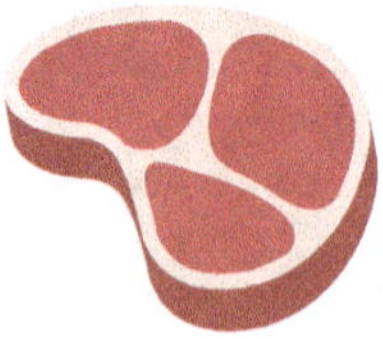

고 기

/go–gi/
meat

구 두 /d/

/gu–du/
dress shoes

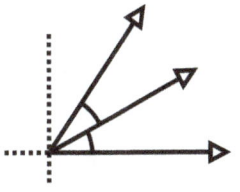

/g<u>ak</u>/
angle

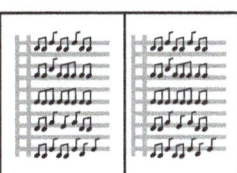

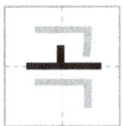

/g<u>ok</u>/
music piece

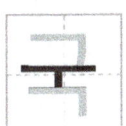

/g<u>uk</u>/
a type of Korean soup

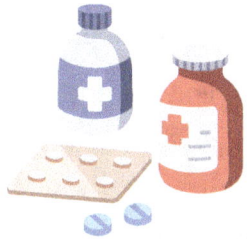

/ya<u>k</u>/
drug, medicine

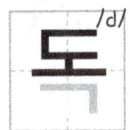

/do<u>k</u>/
poison, venom

/ha<u>k</u>/
crane
(an auspicious animal in Korean culture.)

The sound of ㅋ(*Kieuk*,키읔) is similar to the /k/ in *Kite* or *Kick*. It is an aspirated sound, meaning more air is released during pronunciation, making it stronger than ㄱ.

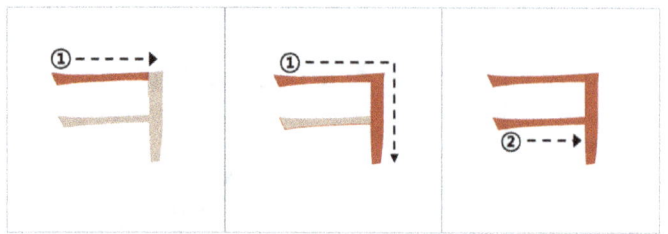

To write ㅋ, start by drawing a ㄱ. Next, add a horizontal line in the middle of it. This middle line should be the same length as, or slightly shorter than, the top horizontal line of the ㄱ.

✎ Trace each letter and see how ㅋ changes its shape with different vowels.

Say the word out loud and trace the ㅋ in the block.

카 드 /d/

/kah—deu/
card

커 피 /p/

/kuh—pi/
coffee

코 트 /t/

/ko—teu/
coat

쿠 키

/ku—ki/
cookie

키

/ki/
height

부 /b/ 엌

/bu—eok/
kitchen

ㄲ
gg,k

Ssang in **Ssang—Giyeok** means "*pair,*" as ㄲ(**Ssang—Giyeok, 쌍기역)** is formed by combining two ㄱs. It represents a tenser, more emphatic version of ㄱ, pronounced as */gg/* with added pressure, similar to the */k/* in *Skate* when said with extra emphasis.

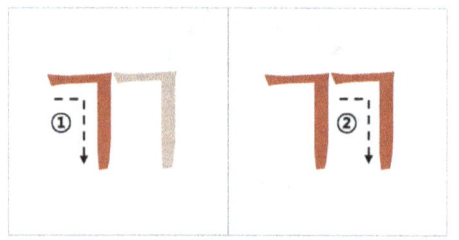

To write ㄲ, draw two small ㄱs side by side. Making the two ㄱs identical, like twins, will give your writing a cleaner and more balanced appearance.

✏️ Trace each letter and see how ㄲ changes its shape with different vowels.

까	꺄	꺼	껴	꼬	꾜
꾸	꾸	끄			

Read the words aloud and trace ㄲ in the syllables below.

가 까 이

/ga—gga—i/
nearby, close

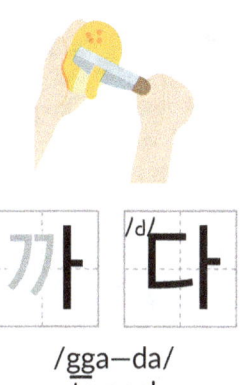

까 /d/다

/gga—da/
to peel

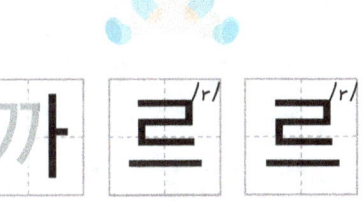

까 르/r/ 르/r/

/gga—reu—reu/
a sound of giggling or laughing out

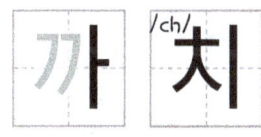

까 치/ch/

/gga—chi/
magpie
(a bird associated
with good luck in Korea)

꼬 리/r/

/ggo—ri/
tail

꼬 마/m/

/ggo—ma/
little kid

DAY 12   ㄷ / ㅌ / ㄸ

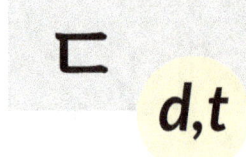

The sound of ㄷ (*Digeut*, 디귿) is similar to the */d/* sound in **D**og or **D**ay, but it is less aspirated. It is pronounced with the tongue lightly touching the ridge behind the upper teeth. At the beginning of a syllable, ㄷ sounds like a soft */d/*. However, when it appears at the end of a syllable, it shifts to a soft */t/* sound.

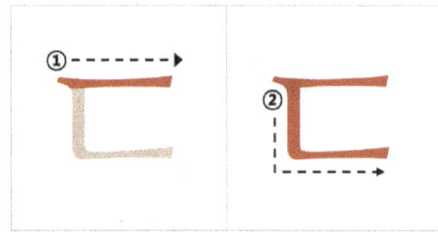

To write ㄷ, draw a horizontal line. Then, starting from the left end of that line, a vertical line going down. Without lifting your pencil, finish with another horizontal line to the right. Keep the two horizontal lines parallel and the same length to make your writing look neat.

✏ Trace each letter and see how ㄷ changes its shape with different vowels.

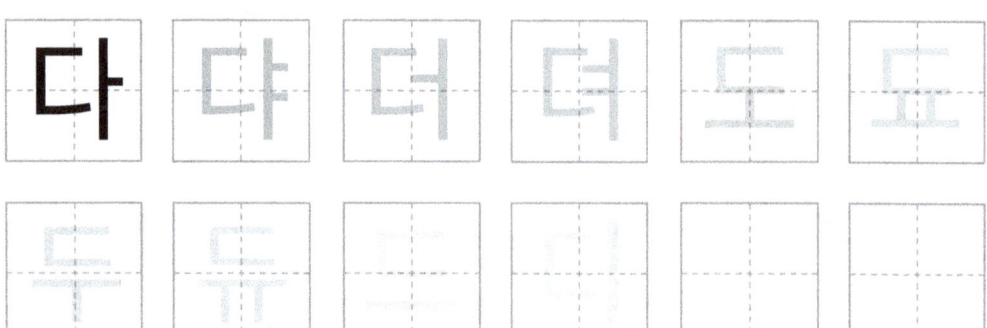

Read the words aloud and trace ㄷ in the syllables below.

다 리 /r/

/da–ri/
leg

도 로 /r/

/do–ro/
road, street

두 더 지 /j/

/du–deo–ji/
mole

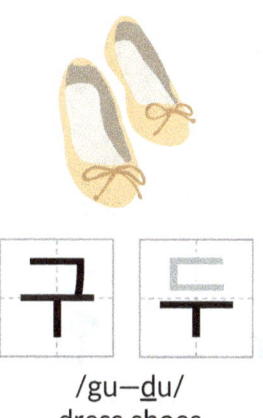

구 두

/gu–du/
dress shoes

두 부 /b/

/du–bu/
tofu

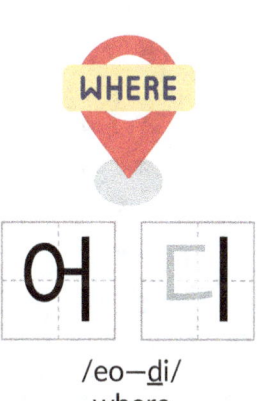

어 디

/eo–di/
where

The sound of ㅌ(*Tieut*,티읕) in Korean is similar to the /t/ sound in **Top** or **Table**. It's a strong, aspirated sound with a burst of air when pronounced.

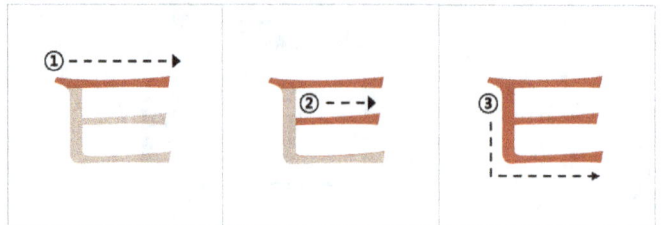

To write ㅌ, draw a horizontal line near the top. Then, draw a second horizontal line parallel to it. Next, starting from the left end of the first line, draw a vertical line downward and finish with another horizontal line to the right—without lifting your pencil. To keep it neat, make sure all the horizontal lines stay parallel.

✏️ Trace each letter and see how ㅌ changes its shape with different vowels.

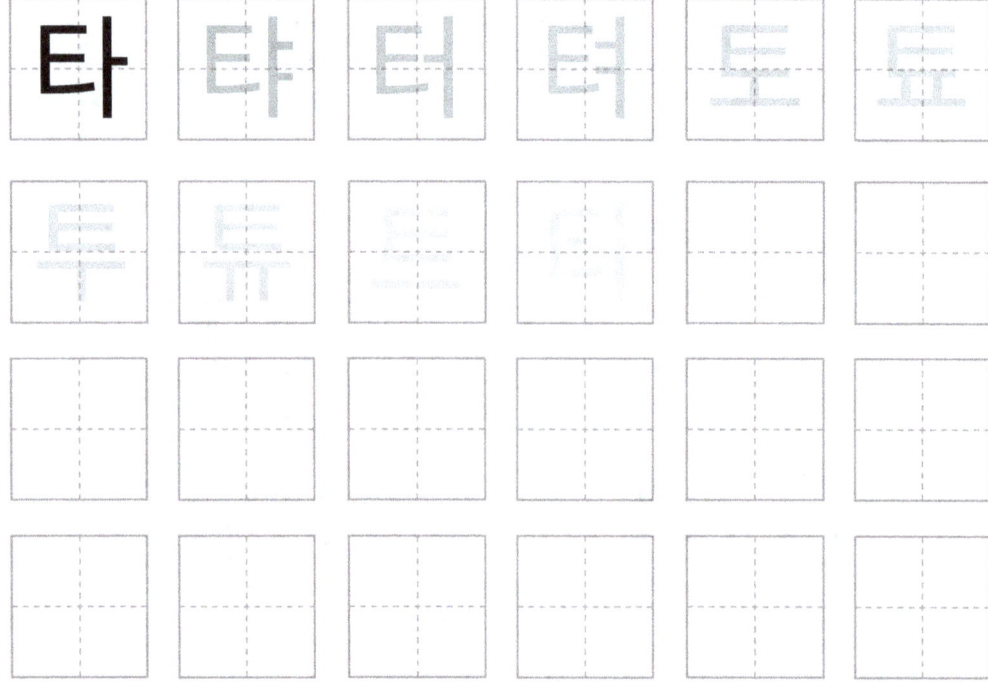

Read the words aloud and trace ㅌ in the syllables below.

타 ^{/j/}조
/t̲a–jo/
ostrich

도 토 ^{/r/}리
/do–t̲o–ri/
acorn

토 ^{/gg/}끼
/t̲o–ggi/
rabbit

티 트 ^{/r/}리
/t̲i–t̲eu–ri/
tea tree

오 타
/o–t̲a/
typo, misspelling

^{/p/}파 티
/pa–t̲i/
party

ㄸ
dd,t

Like ㄲ, ㄸ (*Ssang–Digeut*, 쌍디귿) is formed by combining two ㄷs, meaning "*a pair of Digeuts.*" It represents a tenser version of the ㄷ /d/ sound and is pronounced as /**dd**/ with greater pressure. While there is no exact equivalent in English, it resembles the strong /**tt**/ sound pronounced forcefully in words like S<u>t</u>op. Lastly, the final consonant ㄸ is pronounced with a /t/ sound.

To write ㄸ, draw two small ㄷs side by side. Making the two ㄷs identical, like twins, will give your writing a cleaner and more balanced appearance.

✏ Trace each letter and see how ㄸ changes its shape with different vowels.

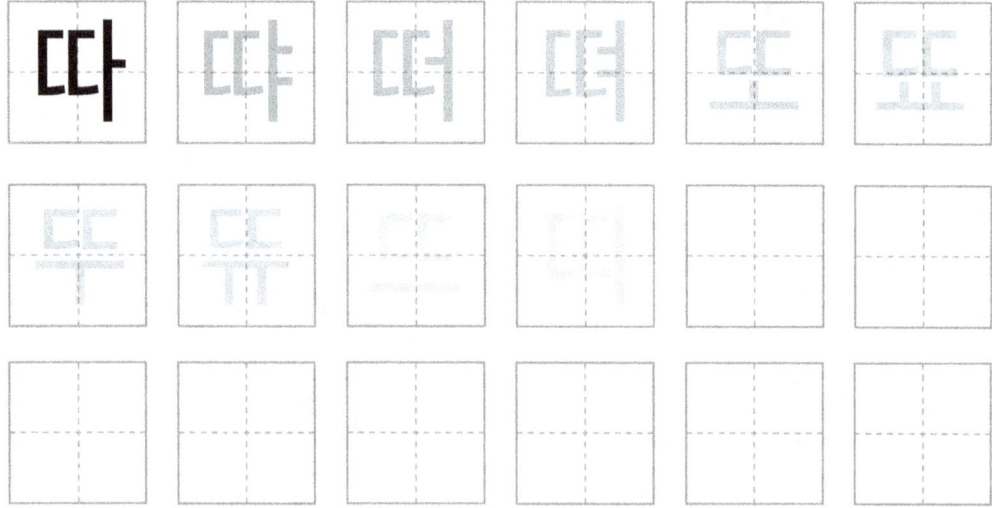

Read the words aloud and trace ㄸ in the syllables below.

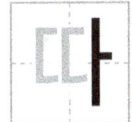

/ddа—ra/
along, following, to mimic

/ddа—ro/
separately, apart

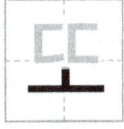

/ddo/
again, also

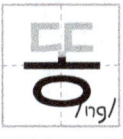

/ddong/
poop

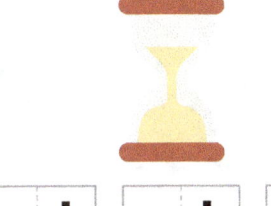

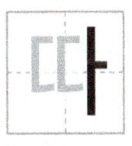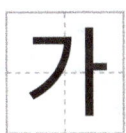

/i—dda—ga/
in several hours

/ddi/
belt, sash

DAY 13

ㅈ / ㅊ / ㅉ

ㅈ
j,t

ㅈ (*Jieut*,지읒) sounds similar to **/j/** in *Jump* or *July*. To pronounce it, lightly press your tongue against the ridge behind your upper teeth and release air gently. At the start of a syllable, it sounds like a soft **/j/**, but at the end of a syllable, it shifts to a soft **/t/** sound.

To write **ㅈ**, start by drawing a horizontal line at the top. From the middle of this line, draw a slightly curved line slanting down to the left. Finally, add another diagonal line slanting to the right, beginning just below the point where the second line started.

✏️ Trace each letter and see how **ㅈ** changes its shape with different vowels.

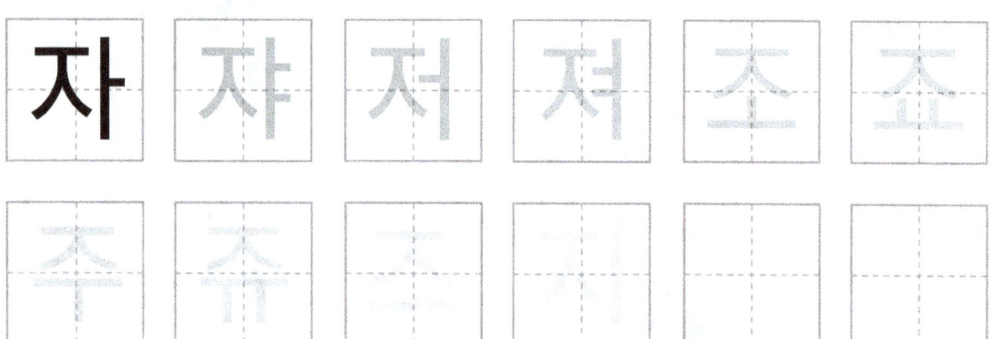

Read the words aloud and trace ㅈ in the syllables below.

자
/ja/
ruler

자 리 /r/
/ja–ri/
seat, spot

주 소 /s/
/jo–so/
address

주 스 /s/
/ju–seu/
juice

지 구
/ji–gu/
Earth, globe

낮
/nat/
daytime

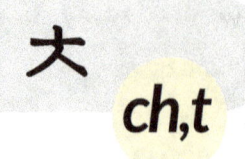

ch,t

ㅊ(*Chieut*,치읓) makes an aspirated /*ch*/ sound, like in <u>*Chair*</u> or <u>*Cheese*</u>. To pronounce it, place your tongue behind your upper teeth and release with more airflow than ㅈ. When ㅊ appears at the end of a syllable, it is pronounced as /*t*/.

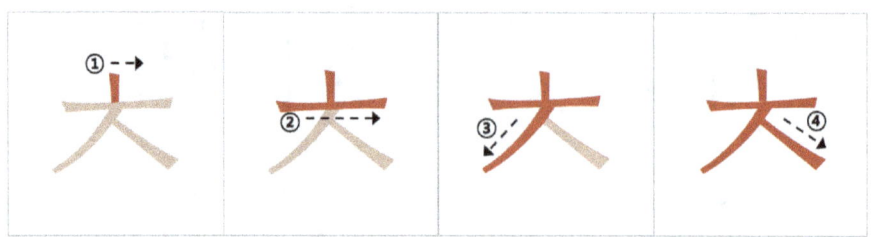

Think of ㅊ as a ㅈ with a hat. Start by drawing the hat first. It can be either a short horizontal or vertical line—choose whichever feels easier. Then, draw ㅈ underneath, making sure the hat lines up with the center of the ㅈ.

Trace each letter and see how ㅊ changes its shape with different vowels.

Read the words aloud and trace ★ in the syllables below.

/cha/
car

차 이

/cha—i/
difference

/cho/
candle

초 보 /b/

/cho—bo/
beginner

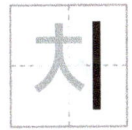 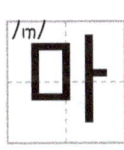 /m/

/chi—ma/
skirt

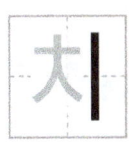 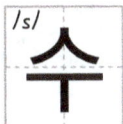 /s/

/chi—su/
size,dimensions

ㅉ **jj,t**

ㅉ(*Ssang—jieut*,쌍지읒) makes a tense /jj/ sound that is stronger and more forceful than ㅈ. To pronounce it, press your tongue firmly against the ridge behind your upper teeth, block the airflow completely, and release it quickly. Since this sound has no direct equivalent in English, listening to Korean words containing ㅉ repeatedly will help you master the pronunciation. Lastly, the batchim ㅉ is pronounced with a /t/ sound

To write ㅉ, draw two small ㅈs side by side. Making the two ㅈs identical, like twins, will give your writing a cleaner and more balanced appearance.

Trace each letter and see how ㅉ changes its shape with different vowels.

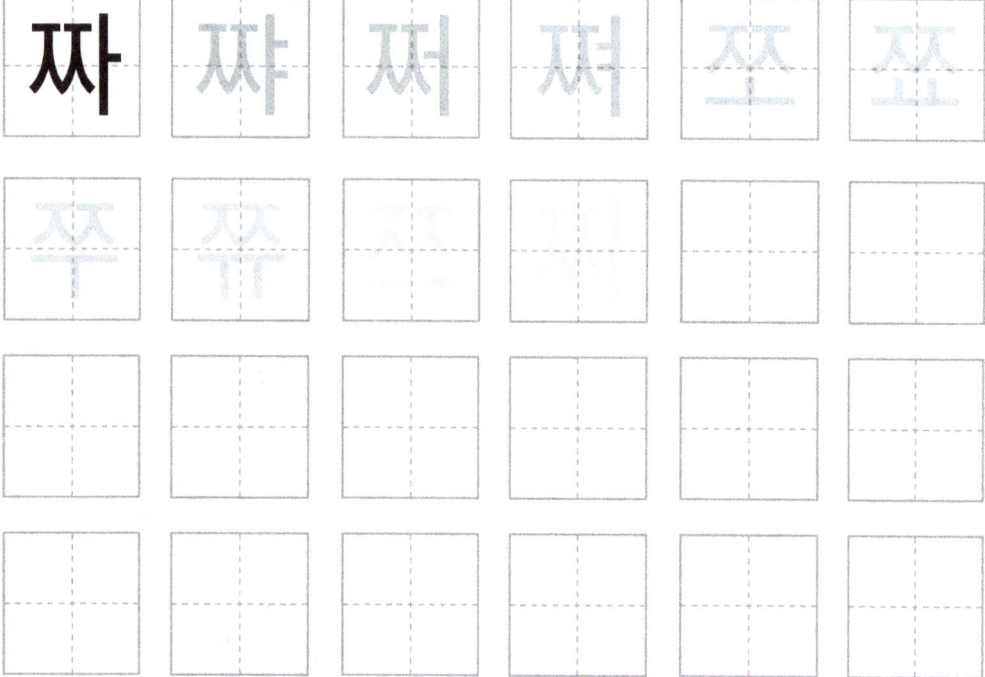

Read the words aloud and trace ㅉ in the syllables below.

짜 다
/jjah–da/
to be salty*

찌 개
/jji–gae/
Korean-style stew

찌 꺼 기
/jji–ggeo–gi/
scraps, remains

가 짜
/ga–jja/
fake

쪼 다
/jjo–da/
to peck at

찌 다
/jji–da/
to steam food

*In Korean, words that modify nouns are called determiners. Unlike English adjectives, Korean determiners can also function as predicates within a sentence.

DAY 14

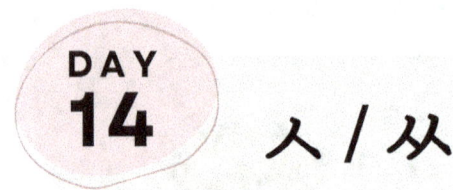
ㅅ / ㅆ

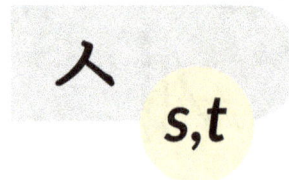
s,t

ㅅ(*Siot*,시옷) makes a soft */s/* sound, similar to the *s* in **Bus**, **Bonus** or **This**. To pronounce it, place your tongue lightly against the roof of your mouth, just behind your upper front teeth, and let air flow out smoothly. At the start of a syllable, ㅅ sounds as */s/*. But when it comes at the end of a syllable, it changes to a */t/* sound.

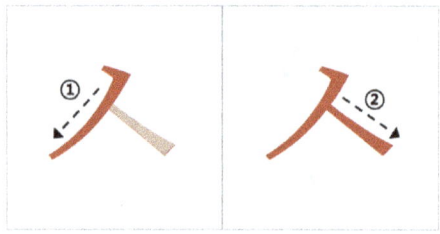

To write ㅅ, draw a diagonal line slanting down to the left. Then, tarting from the top one-third point of the first stroke, draw another diagonal line slanting down to the right.

🖊 Trace each letter and see how ㅅ changes its shape with different vowels.

Read the words aloud and trace ㅅ in the syllables below.

사 고
/s̲a–go/
accident, incident

사 다
/s̲a–da/
to buy, the act of buying

사 이
/s̲a–i/
between, gap

소 리 /r/
/s̲o–ri/
sound

시 소
/s̲i–s̲o/
seesaw

옷
/ot̲/
cloth

ss,t

ㅆ(*Ssang–siot*,쌍시옷) produces a strong /ss/ sound, similar to the crisp *s* in words like **See**, **Sun** or **Song**. It can also resemble the sharp /tsu/ sound found in **Tsunami**. However, when ㅆ appears as a final consonant, it is pronounced as a /t/ sound.

To write ㅆ, draw two small ㅅs side by side. To create space for writing the second ㅅ, draw the short stroke of the first ㅅ shorter than usual.

✏️ Trace each letter and see how ㅆ changes its shape with different vowels.

Read the words aloud and trace ㅆ in the syllables below.

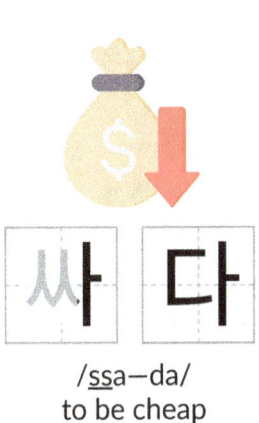

싸 다

/ssa—da/
to be cheap

싸 우 다

/ssa—u—da/
to fight, to argue

쌍 둥 이

/ssang—dung—i/
twins

쏘 다

/sso—da/
to shoot or blast
(colloquially, to cover the bill)

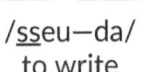

쓰 다

/sseu—da/
to write

있 다

/it—dda*/
there is/are

*If read literally, it would be /it—da/, but due to the sound change rule, /it—dda/ sounds more natural. For more details, see Chapter 6.

DAY 15

ㅂ / ㅍ / ㅃ

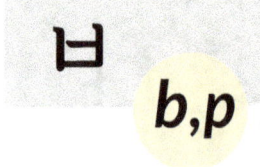

b,p

To pronounce ㅂ(*Bieup*,비읍), begin with your lips lightly pressed together, similar to the *b* sound in *Bat* or *Baby*. When ㅂ comes at the end of a syllable, it sounds more like the *p* in *Cup*, with less airflow.

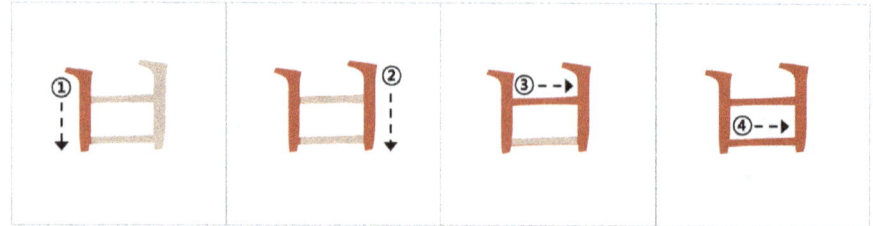

To write ㅂ, draw two parallel vertical lines. Then, connect them with two horizontal lines. To write ㅂ neatly, make sure the horizontal and vertical lines stay straight and parallel.

✏️ Trace each letter and see how ㅂ changes its shape with different vowels.

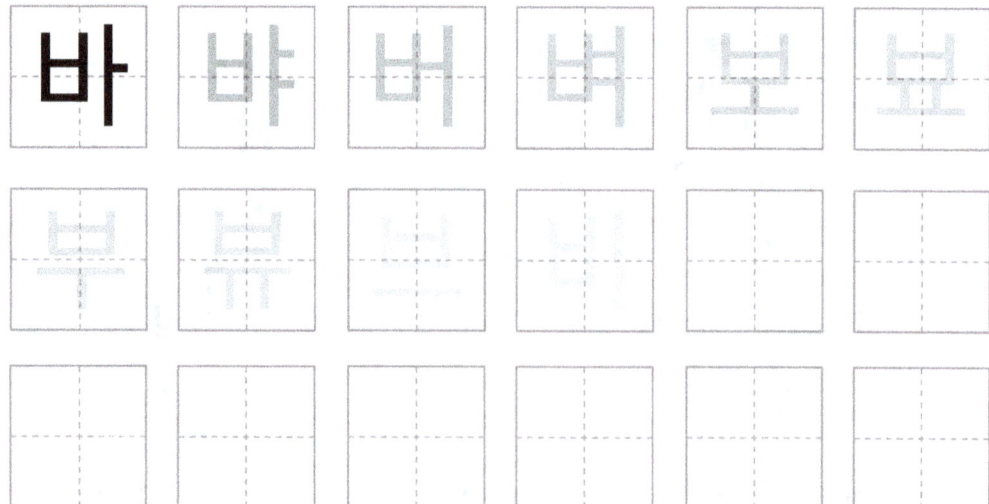

Read the words aloud and trace ㅂ in the syllables below.

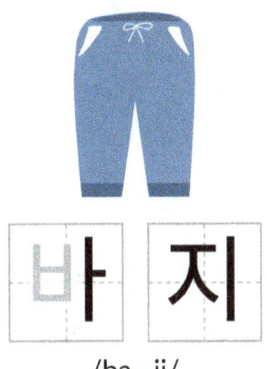

/ba—ji/
pants, trousers

/beo—seu/
bus

/bo—da/
to see, watch, look

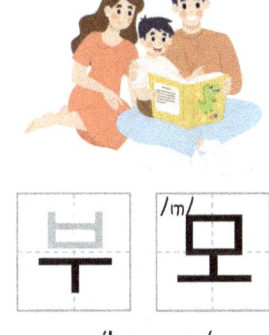

/bu—mo/
parents

/bu—ja/
rich person, the rich

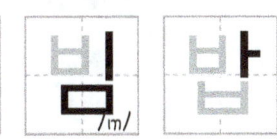

/bi—bim—bap/
Korean mixed rice dish

78

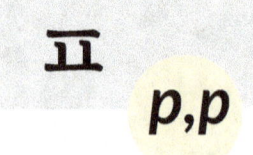

ㅍ(*Pieup*,피읖) is an aspirated consonant. To pronounce it, gently press your lips together, just like when making the ㅂ sound. However, release with a stronger burst of air—similar to the *p* sound in *Pat* or *Person*.

To write ㅍ, start with a horizontal line at the top. Then, write ㅛ beneath it. For neat writing, make sure the top and bottom horizontal lines are equal in length and parallel, while the vertical lines divide the space into three equal parts.

✏ Trace each letter and see how ㅍ changes its shape with different vowels.

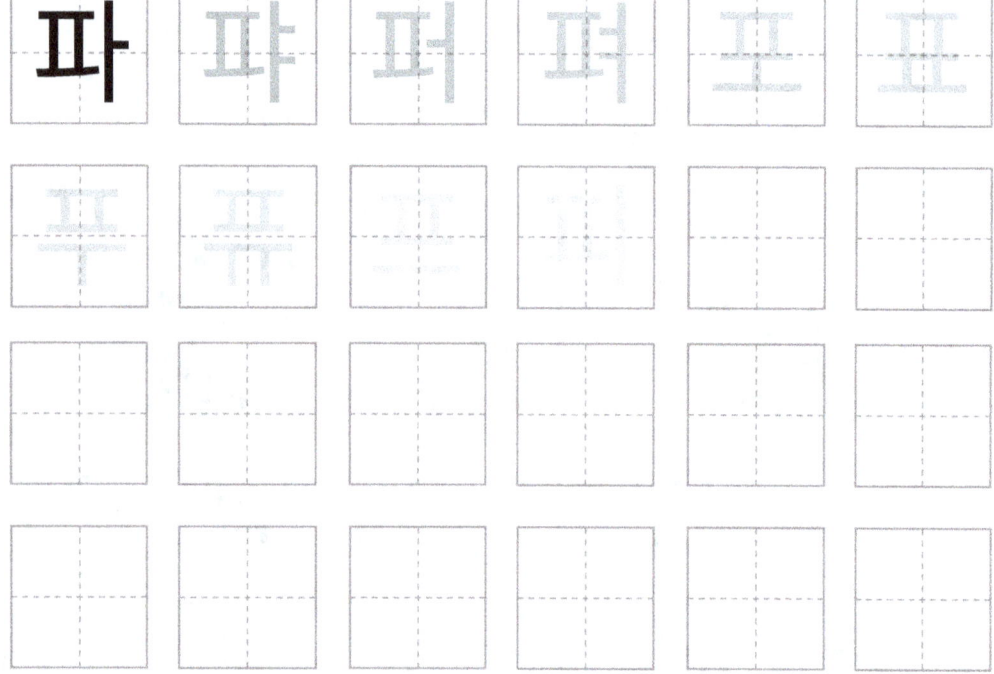

Read the words aloud and trace ㅍ in the syllables below.

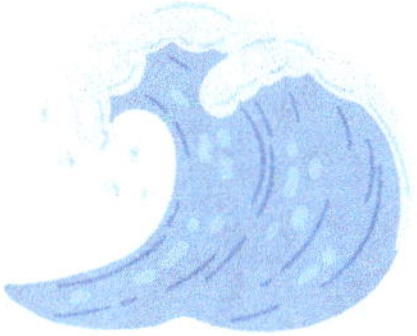

파 도
/p<u>a</u>—d<u>o</u>/
wave

파 리 /r/
/p<u>a</u>—ri/
fly

포 도
/p<u>o</u>—d<u>o</u>/
grape

포 크
/p<u>o</u>—keu/
fork

피 자
/p<u>i</u>—ja/
pizza

잎
/i<u>p</u>/
leaf

ㅃ(*Ssang—bieup*,쌍비읍) represents a tense */bb/* sound, which is stronger and more forceful than the regular */b/* sound of ㅂ. To pronounce ㅃ, press your lips firmly together to block any air from escaping. Then, release them sharply. This produces a crisp, clear sound with more intensity than ㅂ.

To write ㅃ, draw two ㅂs side by side. Like other double consonants, they can be the same size, or make the first one slightly smaller with vertical vowels—both are correct. Choose the style that feels most natural to you.

✏ Trace each letter and see how ㅃ changes its shape with different vowels.

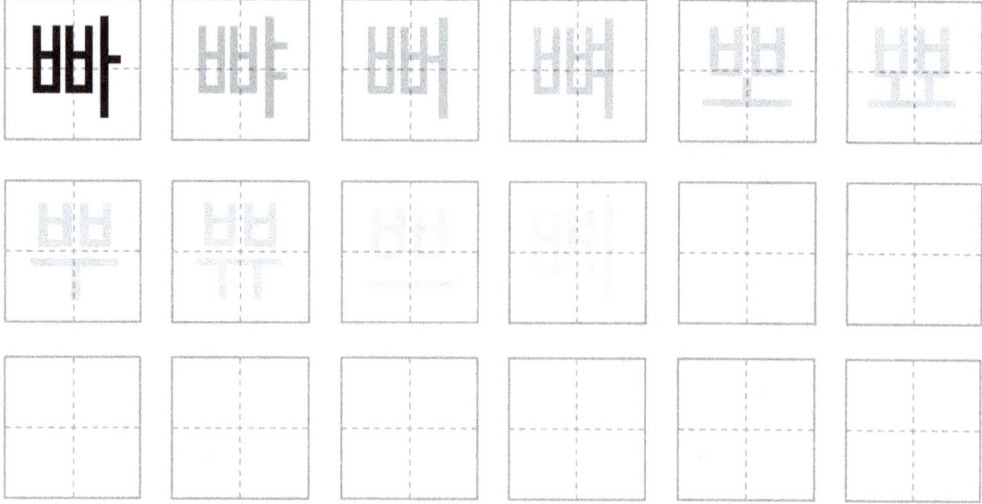

Read the words aloud and trace ㅃ in the syllables below.

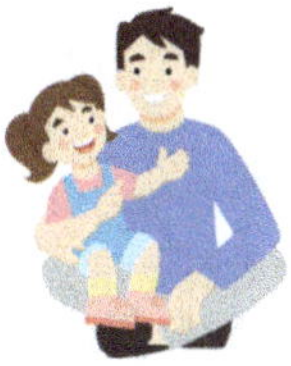

아 빠

/a–bba/
dad

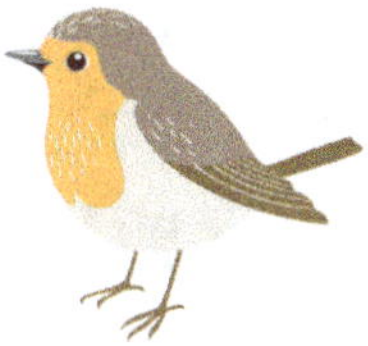

뻐 꾸 기

/bbeo–ggu–gi/
cuckoo

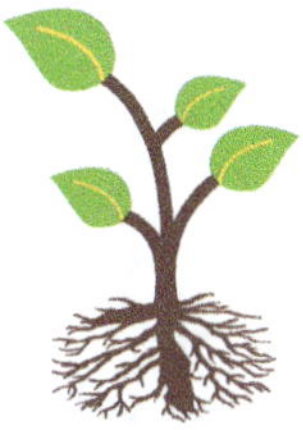

뿌 리 (/r/)

/bbu–ri/
root

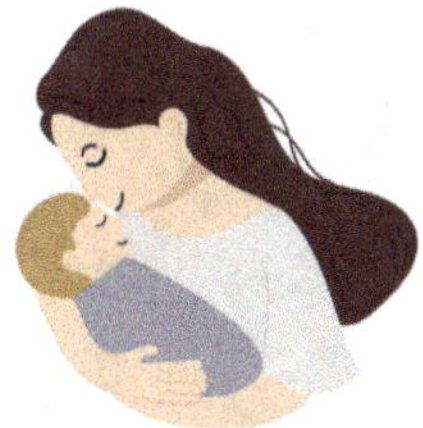

뽀 뽀

/bbo–bbo/
kiss

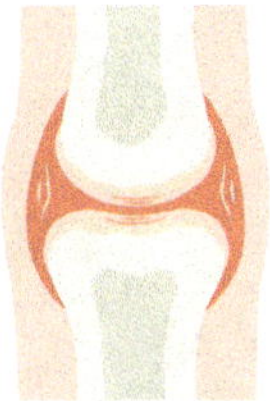

뼈

/bbyeo/
bone

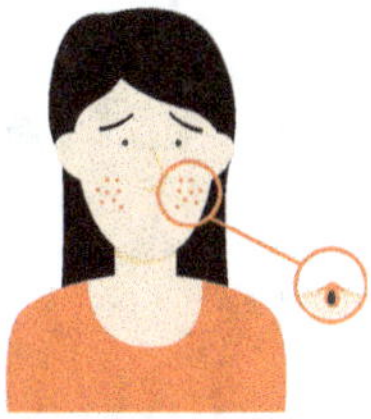

뾰 루 지 (/r/)

/bbyo–ru–ji/
pimple or small bump on the skin

DAY 16

 ㅇ / ㅎ

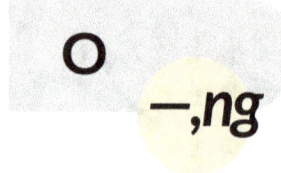 ㅇ
—,ng

The letter ㅇ (*leung*, 이응) has two sounds. At the beginning of a syllable, it serves as a silent placeholder before a vowel, which means that ㅇ is silent in this case. However, when used as a final consonant (batchim), it represents the */ng/* sound.

 To write ㅇ, draw a circle.

✎ Trace each letter and see how ㅇ changes its shape with different vowels.

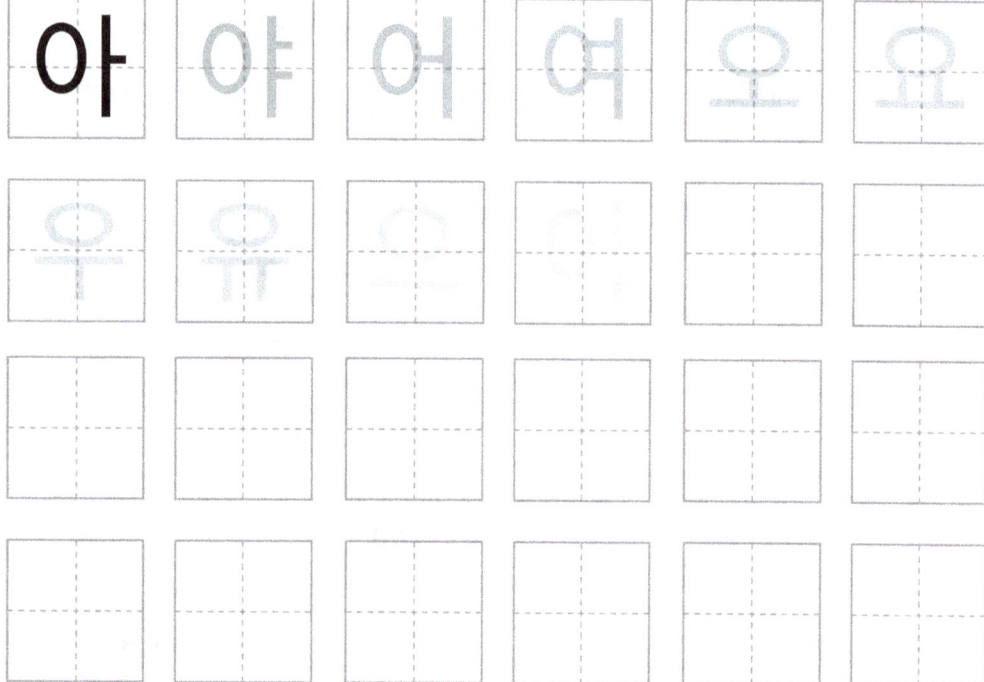

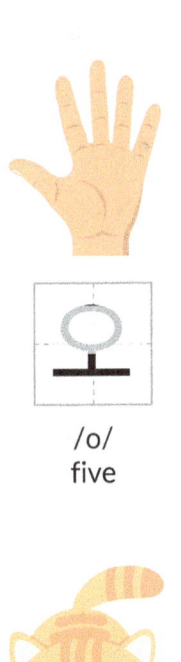

오

/o/
five

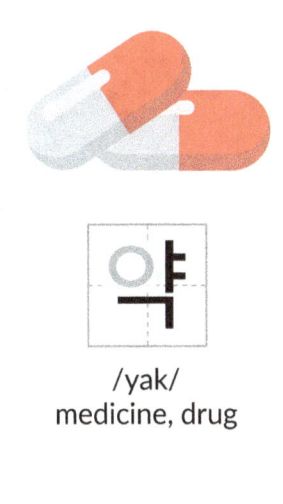

약

/yak/
medicine, drug

고 양 이

/go—yang—i/
cat

우 산

/u—san/
umbrella

안 경

/an—gyeong/
glasses

공

/gong/
ball

ㅎ
h,t

ㅎ (*Hieut*, 히읗) looks like ㅇ wearing a magician's hat, making it easy to remember that ㅎ sounds like **h** in **H**at. However, when ㅎ appears as the batchim, its pronunciation changes depending on the first sound of the next syllable. If the next syllable begins with a consonant, ㅎ typically doesn't make its own sound but influences the following consonant to become aspirated. On the other hand, if the next syllable begins with a vowel (with the silent placeholder ㅇ), ㅎ becomes silent and is not pronounced.

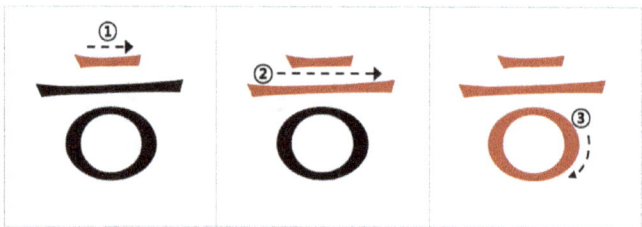

To write ㅎ, draw a short line at the top of the syllable area, ensuring it is centered. Then, draw a longer line beneath it, making sure it aligns with the center of the short line. Finally, place ㅇ directly under the middle of the longer line.

✏ Trace each letter and see how ㅎ changes its shape with different vowels.

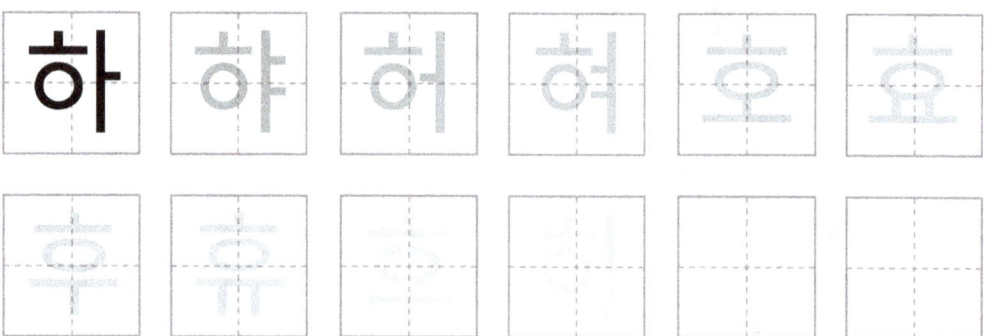

📖 Read the words aloud and trace ㅎ in the syllables below.

하 나 /n/
/ha—na/
one

하 마 /m/
/ha—ma/
hippopotamus

하 루 /r/
/ha—ru/
one day, a day

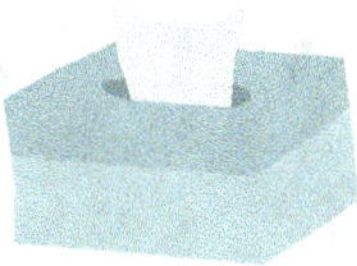

휴 지
/hyu—ji/
tissue,toilet paper

낳 다
/na—ta/*
to have a baby, give birth to, produce

좋 다
/jo—ta/*
to be good

*If read literally, they would be /nat—da/ and /jot—da/, but due to the sound change rule, /na—ta/ and /jo—ta/sound more natural. For more details, see Chapter 6.

DAY 17 ㄴ / ㄹ / ㅁ

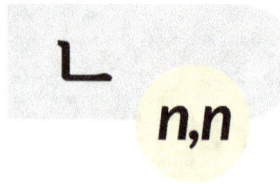

n,n

ㄴ(*Nieun*,니은) is pronounced as /*n*/, similar to the /*n*/ sound in <u>N</u>o or <u>N</u>ice. To produce the sound, place the tip of your tongue just behind your upper front teeth, keeping it inside your mouth, and release it gently.

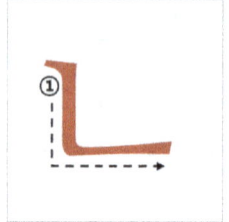

To write ㄴ, draw a vertical line down the left side of the syllable space. Without lifting your pencil, continue into a horizontal line to the right.

✏ Trace each letter and see how ㄴ changes its shape with different vowels.

87

Read the words aloud and trace ㄴ in the syllables below.

나 무 /m/

/na–mu/
tree, wood

나 라 /r/

/na–ra/
country, nation

나 이

/na–i/
age

누 나

/nu–na/
older sister
(used by males)

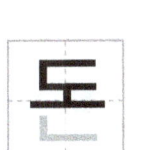

도

/don/
money

산

/san/
mountain

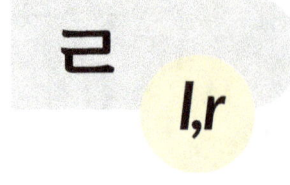

ㄹ

l,r

Korean doesn't distinguish between the /l/ and /r/ sounds because they don't exist separately in the language. Instead, the sound of ㄹ(*Rieul*,리을) is a blend of the English /l/ and /r/ sounds. It doesn't perfectly match either one but falls somewhere in between. Its pronunciation shifts depending on its position in a word and its interaction with the surrounding syllables.

ㄹ is shaped like a flattened combination of ㄱ and ㄴ, with a horizontal line in the middle. To write ㄹ, begin by writing ㄱ, then add a horizontal line equal in length to the top stroke of ㄱ. Finally, write ㄴ of the same size as ㄱ below the horizontal line.

✏️ Trace each letter and see how ㄹ changes its shape with different vowels.

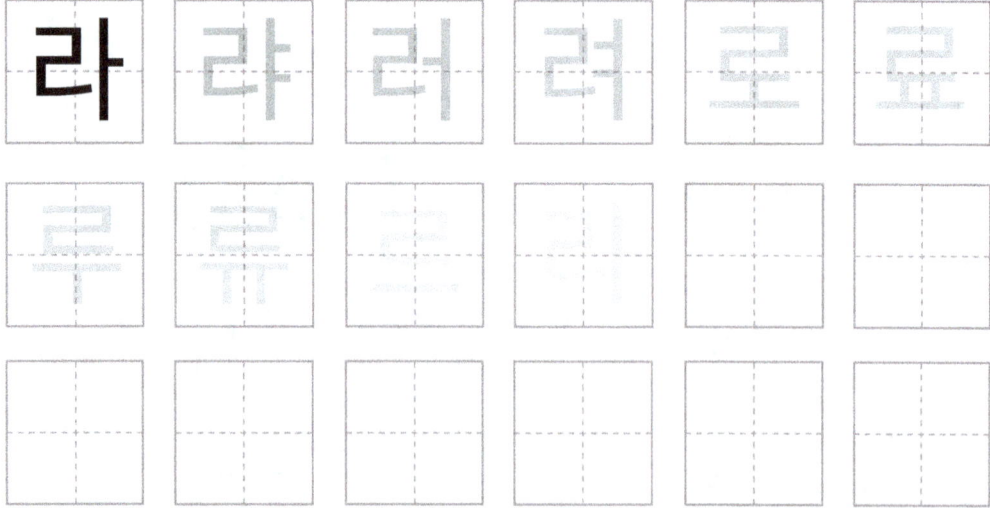

Read the words aloud and trace ㄹ in the syllables below.

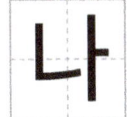 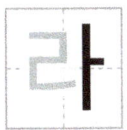

/na—ra/
country, nation

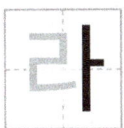 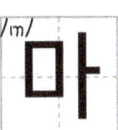

/la—ma/
llama

  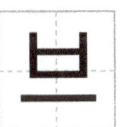

/la—i—beu/
live streaming
(as in live performance,
live broadcast, etc.)

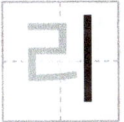 

/li—deo/
leader

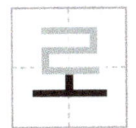 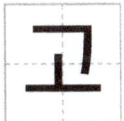

/lo—go/
logo

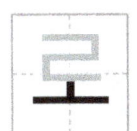 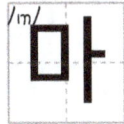

/lo—ma/
Rome

Understanding the Pronunciation of ㄹ

A. When ㄹ sounds more like the English /l/

- When it is the <u>initial consonant of the first syllable in a word</u> or <u>the batchim (final consonant) of any syllable</u>.

- When two ㄹ appear consecutively across two syllables, they are both pronounced more like /l/ than /r/.

달리기
/dal—li—gi/
(running)

루돌프
/lu—dol—peu/
(rudolph)

B. When ㄹ sounds more like the English /r/

- Most other cases.

- It doesn't matter whether the original loanword starts with *l* or *r*.

오로라
/o—ro—ra/
(aurora)

로그인
/ro—geu—in/
(login)

m,m

ㅁ(*Mieum*,미음) is similar to the */m/* sound in words like _Mom_ or _Moon_. To pronounce it, close your lips completely and let the sound resonate through your nose. It is a soft nasal sound.

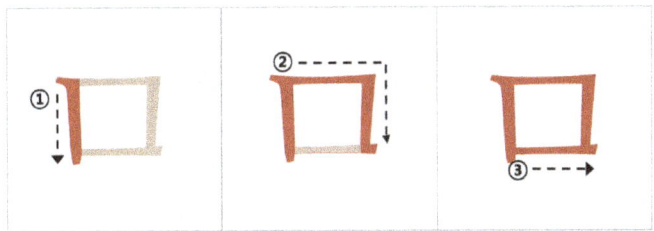

ㅁ looks like a simple square. However, depending on its position, ㅁ may appear wider horizontally or taller vertically, but the stroke order never changes. First, draw a vertical line. Next, add ㄱ, starting from the top of the first line. Finally, connect the bottoms of the two vertical lines with a horizontal line. To keep your ㅁ neat, make sure the horizontal lines stay parallel to each other, and the vertical lines stay parallel to each other.

✎ Trace each letter and see how ㅁ changes its shape with different vowels.

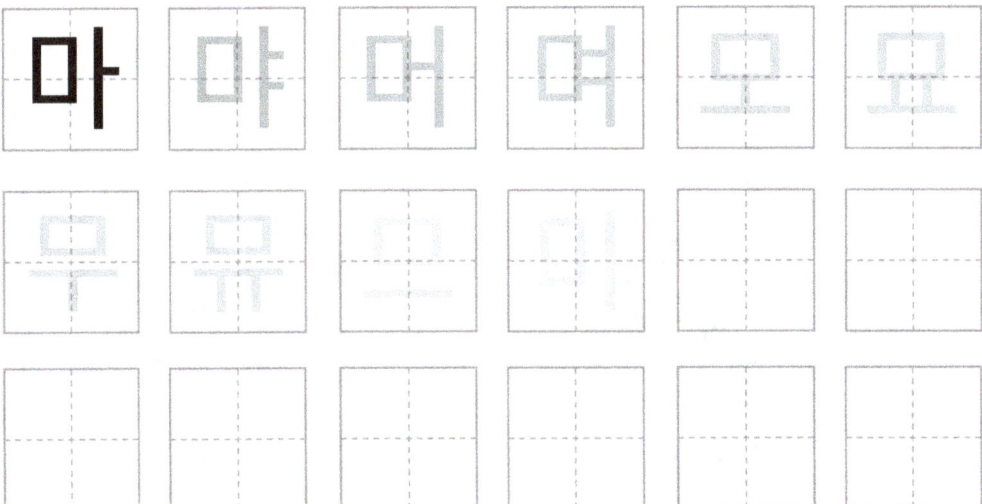

Read the words aloud and trace ▫ in the syllables below.

/<u>m</u>a–ru/
flooring, floor materials

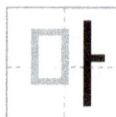 

/<u>m</u>a–ri/
counter for animals

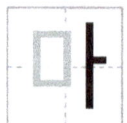 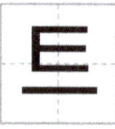

/<u>m</u>a–teu/
mart, supermarket

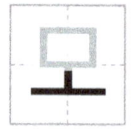 

/<u>m</u>o–ja/
hat

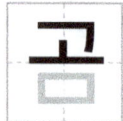

/go<u>m</u>/
bear

몸

/<u>m</u>o<u>m</u>/
body

Practice writing Hangul in any way you like!

Chapter 04

이중모음
DOUBLE VOWELS

SCAN ME!

DAY 18 · Double Vowels

11 Double Vowels

In this chapter, we will explore double vowels, which are formed by combining two basic vowels. Their pronunciation flows smoothly, blending the two vowels into a single sound. Double vowels are divided into two groups: the *Vertical Double Vowels*, which consist only of vertical vowels, and the *Complex Double Vowels*, which combine vertical and horizontal vowels.

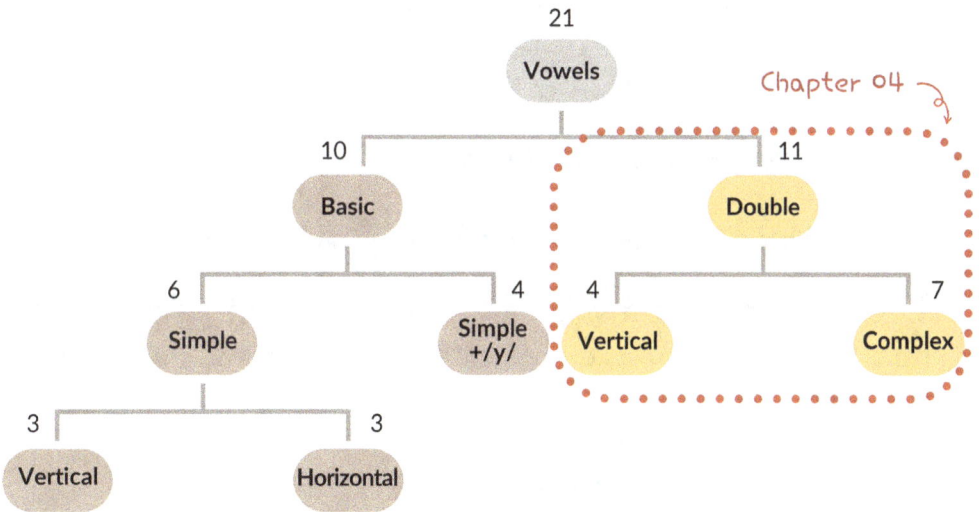

Intuitive Classification of the 21 Hangul Vowels
(Numbers Indicate Total Count)

A complex vowel is also referred to as a combined vowel.

The two groups are composed as follows:

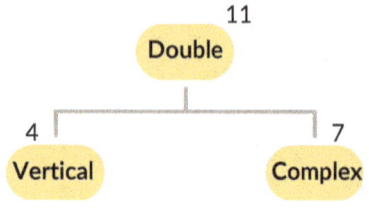

- Vertical Double Vowels: ㅐ,ㅔ,ㅒ,ㅖ. made up of only vertical vowels.
- Complex Double vowels: ㅞ,ㅙ,ㅚ,ㅘ,ㅝ,ㅟ,ㅢ. made up of a mix of vertical and horizontal component

Additionally, pay attention to the sounds created when two basic vowels combine, such as ㅘ and ㅞ. These combinations may slightly change the original sounds. For instance, ㅗ alone is pronounced /o/, and ㅜ is /u/. But when combined with another vowel, they often take on a /w/-like sound, resulting in a smoother, more natural pronunciation.

A Double Vowel's Position Within a Syllable

Vertical double vowels are placed in the same way as other vertical vowels. The following examples are taken from Chapter 1, Letter Placement Within a Syllable. For additional practice, review sections A-3 and B-3.

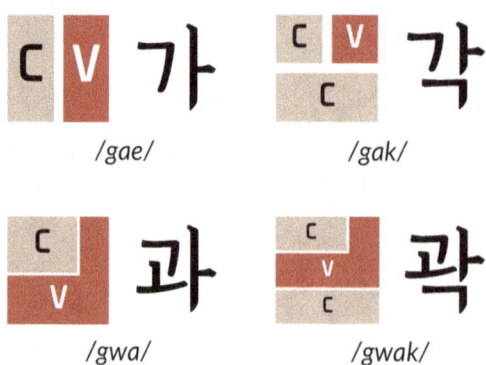

/gae/   /gak/

/gwa/   /gwak/

The tables below summarize all 11 double vowels in Korean. While their pronunciation notations follow official guidelines, we've made a few adjustments to make them easier to understand and use in everyday conversation. For example, the official system distinguishes between ㅐ (/ae/) and ㅔ (/e/). Here, we simply use /ae/ for both, since they sound almost identical and are rarely distinguished in casual speech. Similar simplifications are applied to vowels such as ㅙ, ㅞ, and ㅚ.

As we mentioned before, try not to depend too much on phonetic symbols. Some sounds can be especially tricky for learners—for instance, ㅢ, which many non-native speakers find difficult to master. Instead of relying solely on symbols, the best way to improve is by listening and practicing speaking.

11 Double Vowels

	Category	Letter	Pronunciation	Shape
11 Double Vowels	Vertical	ㅐ	/ae/	ㅏ + ㅣ
		ㅔ		ㅓ + ㅣ
		ㅒ	/yae/	ㅑ + ㅣ
		ㅖ		ㅕ + ㅣ
	Complex (vertical+ horizontal)	ㅙ	/wae/	ㅗ + ㅐ
		ㅞ		ㅜ + ㅐ
		ㅚ		ㅗ + ㅣ

	Category	Letter	Pronunciation	Shape
11 **Double** **Vowels**	Complex (vertical+ horizontal)	ᅪ	/wa/	ㅗ+ㅏ
		ᅯ	/wo/	ㅜ+ㅓ
		ᅱ	/wi/	ㅜ+ㅣ
		ᅴ	/eui/	ㅡ+ㅣ

Two Short Strokes Add a /y/ Sound

In Korean vowels, two short strokes indicate a **/y/** sound—just think of ㅑ, ㅕ, ㅛ, and ㅠ. This rule also applies to vertical double vowels.

Vertical double vowel sounds fall into two types: **/ae/** and **/yae/**. When the vowel includes ㅏ or ㅓ, it's pronounced **/ae/**. But if it includes ㅑ or ㅕ, a **/y/** sound is added, making it **/yae/**.

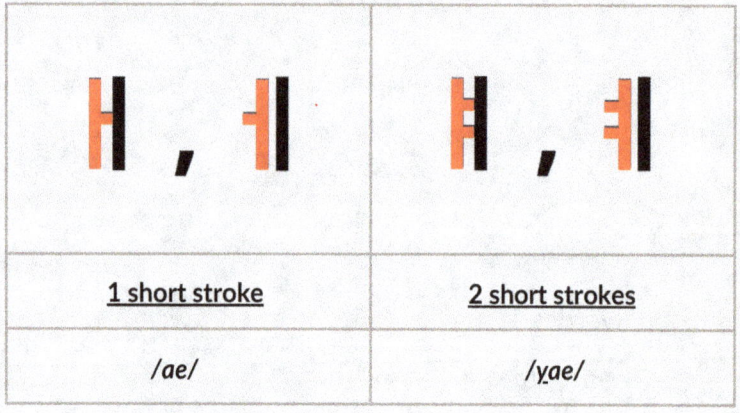

1 short stroke	2 short strokes
/ae/	/yae/

DAY 19

ㅐ / ㅔ

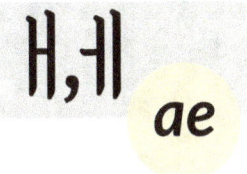

ㅐ,ㅔ
ae

The vowels ㅐ and ㅔ produce very similar sounds, both resembling the short /ɛ/ in the English word **B_ed_**, with only subtle differences that can be hard to notice.

In modern Korean conversation, speakers do not clearly distinguish between these sounds in pronunciation. However, in the past, their pronunciations were distinct: ㅐ was pronounced with a more open mouth and a lower tongue position, similar to the /æ/ sound in bad. In contrast, ㅔ was pronounced with the mouth slightly more closed and the tongue positioned slightly higher, resembling the /ɛ/ sound in bed.

Both letters are written with two vertical strokes and one horizontal stroke. The difference is which you write first: ㅏ or ㅓ.

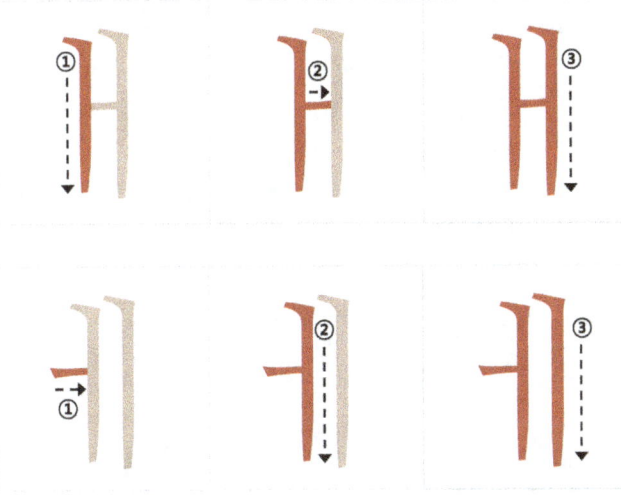

To write ㅐ, start with ㅏ and then add ㅣ to its right. To write ㅔ, start with ㅓ and then add ㅣ to its right.

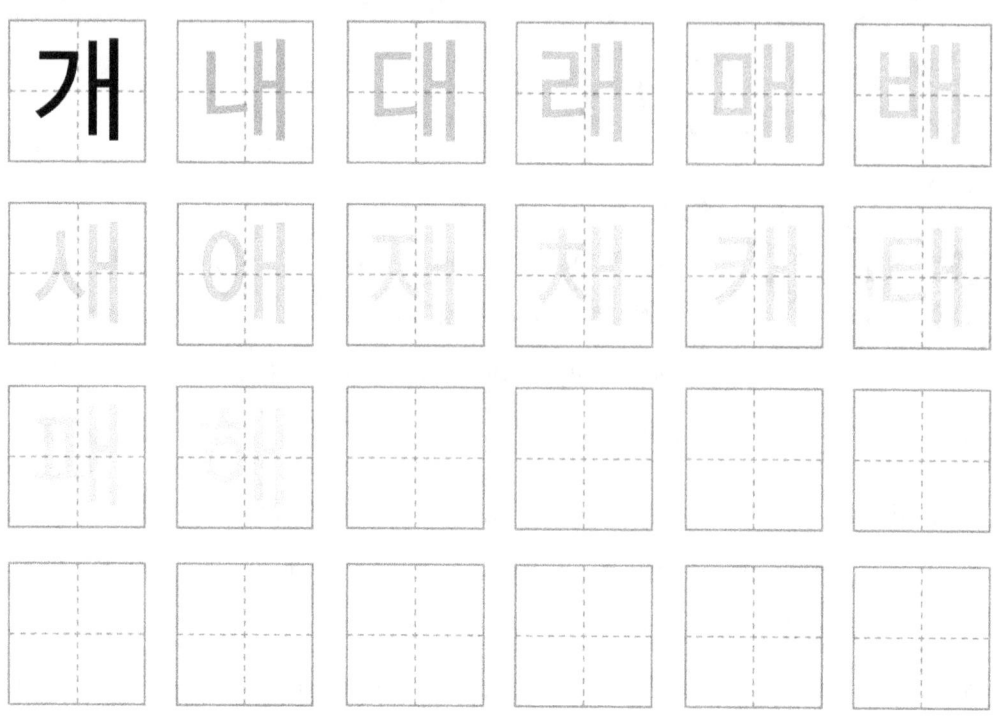

Follow the correct writing order as you trace ㅔ.

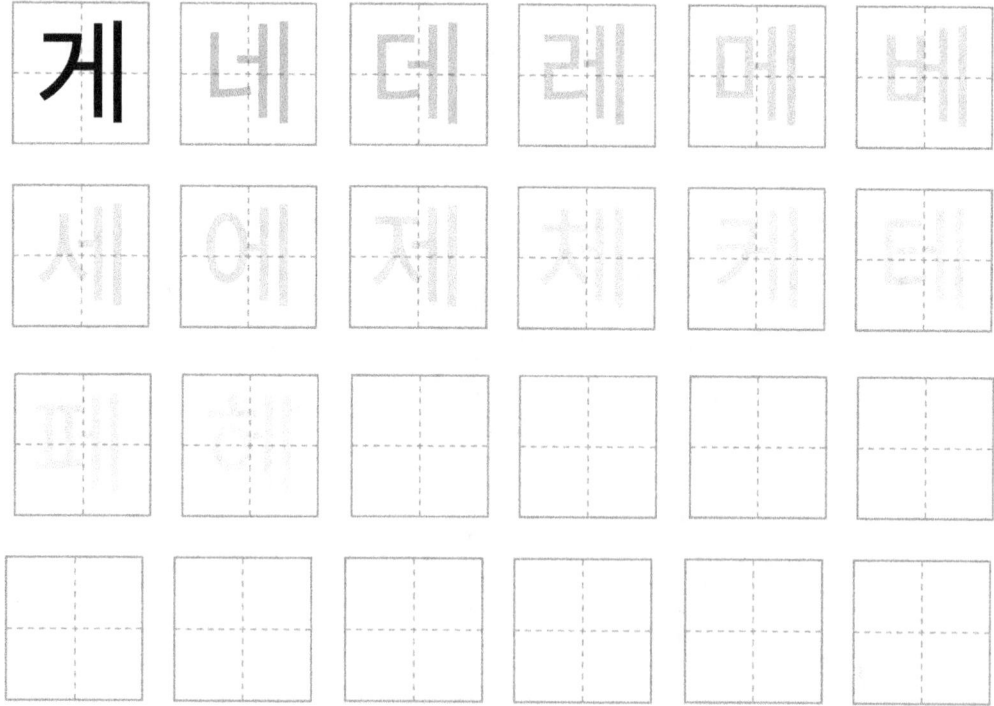

Read the words aloud and trace ㅐ in the syllables below.

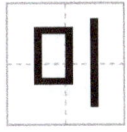

/g<u>ae</u>—mi/
ant

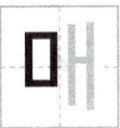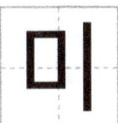

/m<u>ae</u>—mi/
cicada

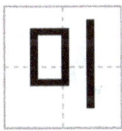

/j<u>ae</u>—mi/
fun, interest

/jo—g<u>ae</u>/
seashell

/s<u>ae</u>/
bird

/ch<u>ae</u>k/
book

Read the words aloud and trace ㅔ in the syllables below.

/ga—<u>gae</u>/
store

그 네

/geu—n<u>ae</u>/
swing

/b<u>ae</u>—gae/
pillow

세 수

/s<u>ae</u>—su/
face washing

게 임

/<u>gae</u>—im/
game

숙 제

/suk—<u>jae</u>/
homework

DAY 20

ㅒ / ㅖ

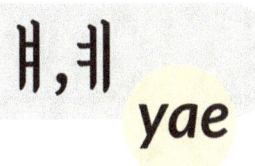

ㅒ, ㅖ
yae

The vowels ㅒ and ㅖ produce very similar sounds, both resembling the short /ye/ in the English word **Yes**, with only subtle differences that can be hard to notice.

In the past, ㅒ and ㅖ were pronounced differently. The sound ㅒ followed this pattern: ㅏ → ㅑ → ㅒ, while ㅖ followed ㅓ → ㅕ → ㅖ. The main difference between these two sounds lies in the position of the tongue and the degree of mouth opening:

- For ㅒ, the tongue was positioned farther forward, and the mouth opened wider.
- For ㅖ, the tongue moved farther back, and the mouth was slightly less open.

IIn modern Korean, it's fine to pronounce these two sounds the same. Still, note the difference in usage: ㅖ often appears in words of Chinese origin, while ㅒ does not.

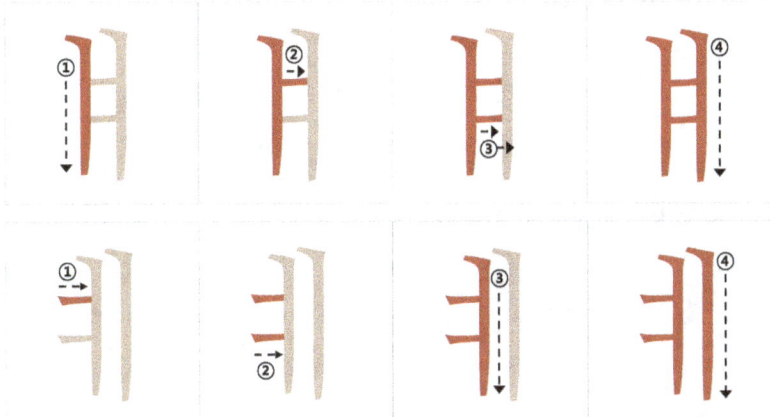

Both letters are written with two vertical strokes and two horizontal stroke. The difference is which you write first: To write ㅐ, start with ㅏ and then add ㅣ to its right. To write ㅔ, start with ㅓ and then add ㅣ to its right.

✏ Follow the correct writing order as you trace ㅐ.

개	내	대	래	매	배
새	애	재	채	캐	태
패	해				

✏ Follow the correct writing order as you trace ㅔ.

계	녜	뎨	례	메	볘

세 에 제 체 켸 테

페 혜

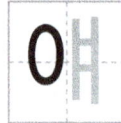

/yae/
an informal way of
referring to "this guy(kid)"
(*abbreviation of* 이 애)

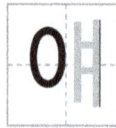 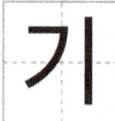

/yae-gi/
story, conversation
(*abbreviation of* 이야기)

 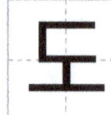 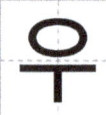

/syae-do-wu/
eye shadow

/ha-yae-ji-da/
to turn white or to become white, the activity of being white

Read the words aloud and trace ㅒ in the syllables below.

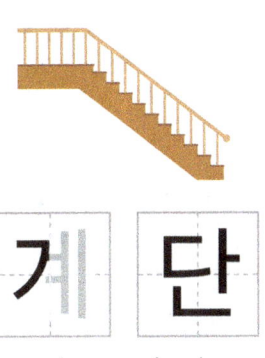

계 단

/gyae–dan/
stairs, steps

단 계

/dan–gyae/
stage, level

시 계

/si–gyae/
clock

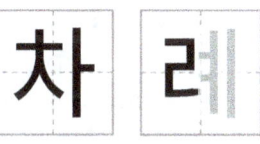

차 례

/cha–ryae/
order, turn, or sequence

예 술

/yae–sul/
art

예 약

/yae–yak/
booking, reservation

DAY 21 ᅫ / ᅰ / ᅬ

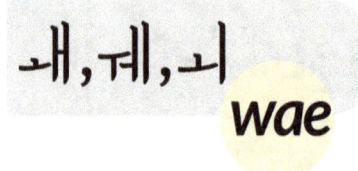
wae

The three vowels produce very similar sounds, both resembling the short */we/* in the English word *Way*, with only subtle differences that can be hard to notice.

Here's how these subtle differences can be recognized.

- ᅫ: Start with ㅗ and quickly add ㅐ.
- ᅰ: Start with ㅜ and quickly add ㅔ.
- ᅬ: This sound is similar to the French *œ*. To pronounce it, shape your mouth as if you're saying ㅗ, but produce the sound ㅣ instead.

However, like ㅐ and ㅔ, in modern Korean, it is acceptable to pronounce ᅫ, ᅰ, and ᅬ the same way. Even Koreans don't always clearly distinguish them in daily conversation.

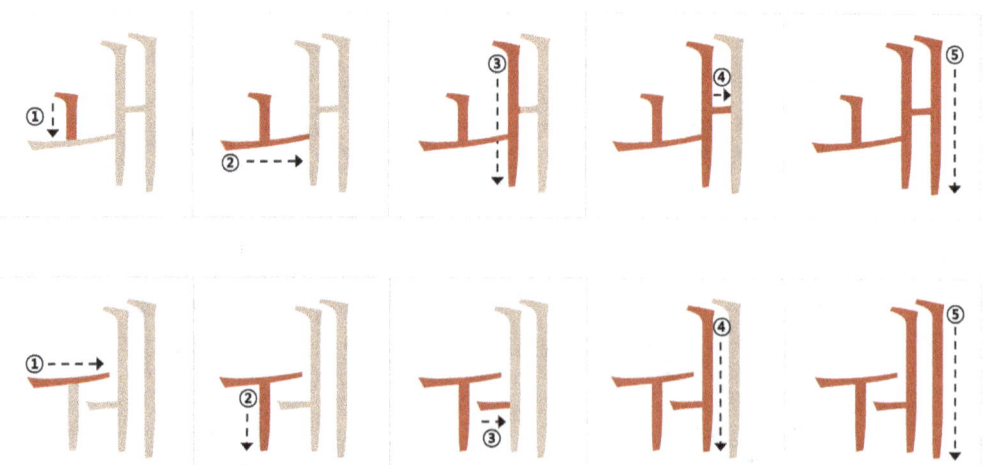

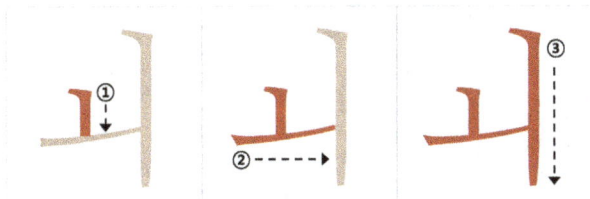

To write ㅙ, start with ㅗ and add ㅐ to the right. To write ㅞ, start with ㅜ and add ㅔ to the right. To write ㅚ, start with ㅗ and add ㅣ to the right.

✏️ Follow the correct writing order as you trace ㅙ.

괘	놰	돼	뢔	뫠	봬
쇄	왜	좨	쵀	쾌	퇔
퐤	횃				

110

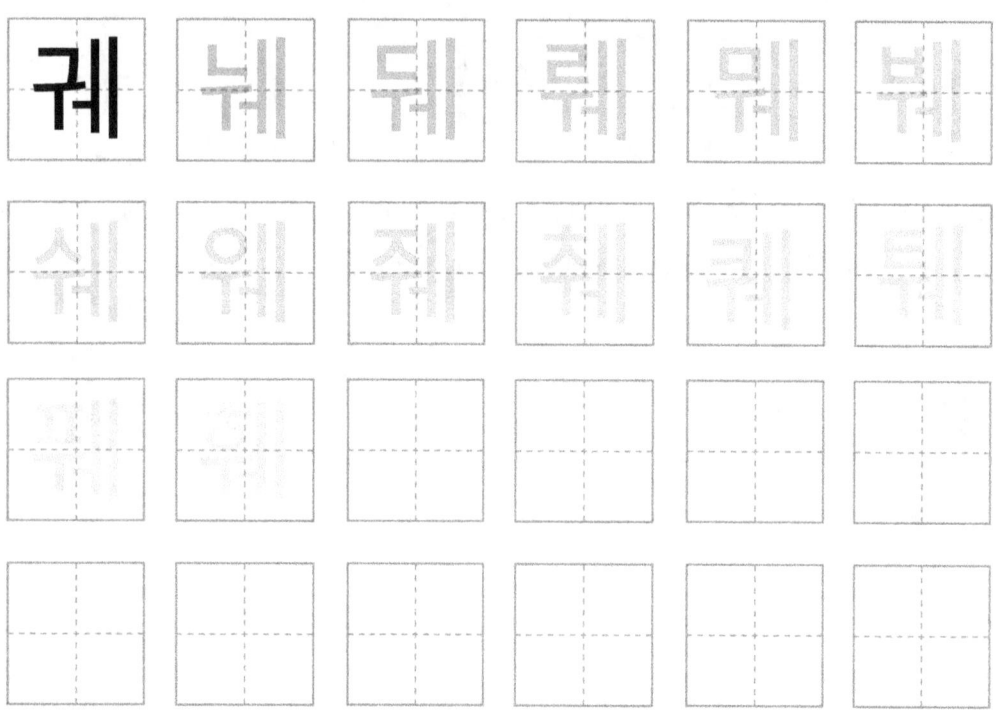

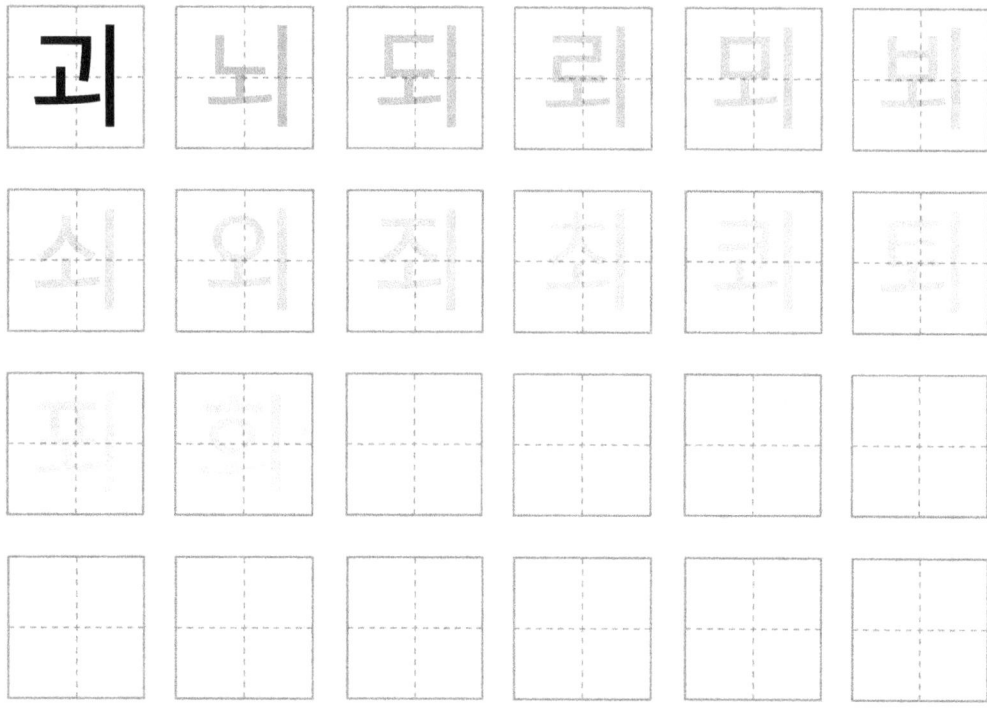

Read the words aloud and trace ㅙ in the syllables below.

/wae/
why

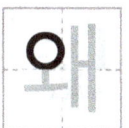 

/wae—so/
small, petite

/dwae—ji/
pig

/hwaet—bul/
torch

 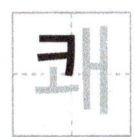

/sang—kwae/
refreshing

/in—swae/
printing

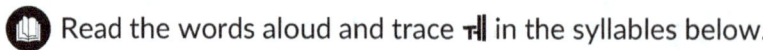 Read the words aloud and trace 궤 in the syllables below.

궤 도

/<u>gwae</u>—do/
orbit, track

스 웨 덴

/seu—<u>wae</u>—daen/
sweden

스 웨 터

/seu—<u>wae</u>—teo/
sweater, knitwear

웨 하 스

/<u>wae</u>—ha—seu/
wafer

웨 이 브

/<u>wae</u>—ee—beu/
wavy and curly hairstyles
(also refer to a body wave dance move)

 훼 손

/<u>hwae</u>—son/
damage, defamation

/gi—h<u>wae</u>/
chance, opportunity

/sa—h<u>wae</u>/
society

 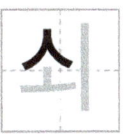

/yeol—s<u>wae</u>/
key

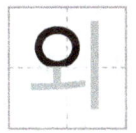 

/<u>wae</u>—tu/
outwear, overcoat

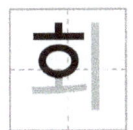 

/h<u>wae</u>—sa/
company, corporation

/gyo—h<u>wae</u>/
church

DAY 22

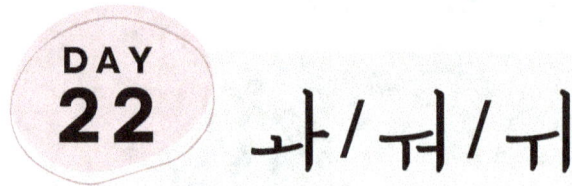

와 / 궈 / 귀

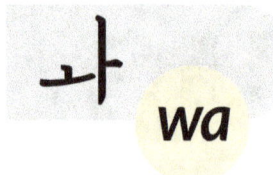

와 is a combination of the vowels ㅗ and ㅏ, showing how the two sounds are connected. To pronounce 와, start by rounding your lips to make the ㅗ sound, and then quickly transition to the ㅏ sound. It creates a smooth, flowing sound identical to /wa/ in *Wallaby*.

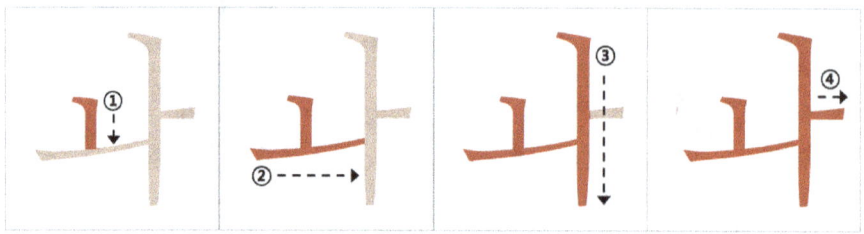

To write 와, start with ㅗ and then add ㅏ to its right.

✏️ Follow the correct writing order as you trace 와.

Read the words aloud and trace ㅘ in the syllables below.

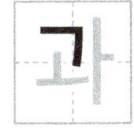 

/gwa–ja/
confection, chips, crackers

/wang/
king

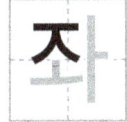 

/jwa–wu/
left and right

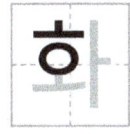 

/hwa–jang/
makeup, cosmetics

/hwan–ja/
patient

/sa–gwa/
apple

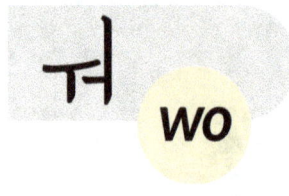

WO

The vowel ㅝ is a combination of ㅜ and ㅓ. To pronounce ㅝ, begin by rounding your lips to make the ㅜ sound, like the /oo/ in **goose**, and then smoothly transition to the ㅓ sound, similar to the *u* in **Cup**. This creates a flowing sound, like the /wo/ in **Wonder**.

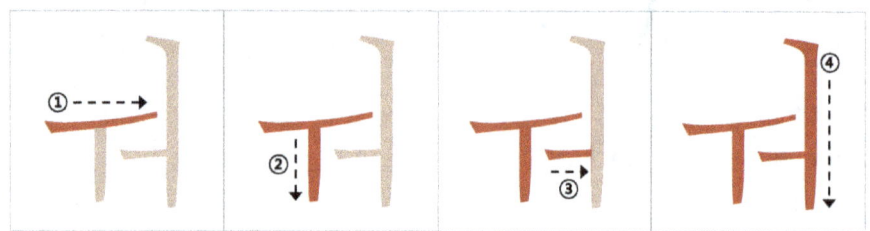

To write ㅝ, start with ㅜ and then add ㅓ to its right.

✏️ Follow the correct writing order as you trace ㅝ.

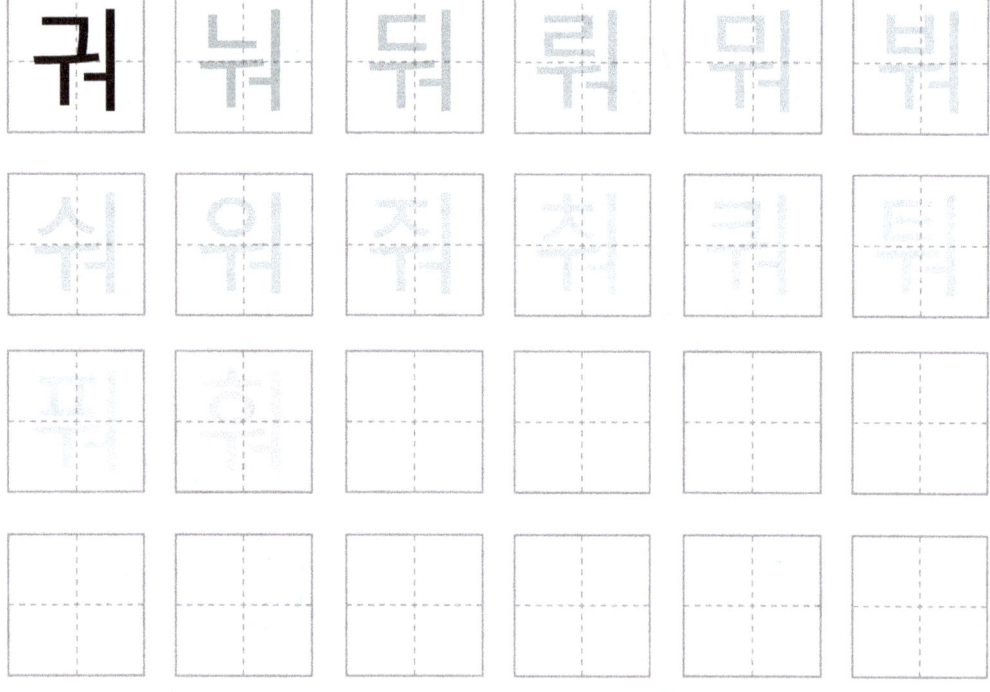

Read the words aloud and trace ㅝ in the syllables below.

공 원

/gong—won/
park

소 원

/so—won/
wish

 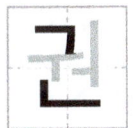

여 권

/yeo—gwon/
passport

원 숭 이

/won—soong—i/
monkey

 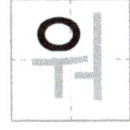

타 워

/ta—wo/
tower

 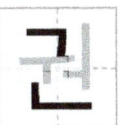 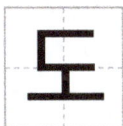

태 권 도

/tae—gwon—do/
Taekwondo

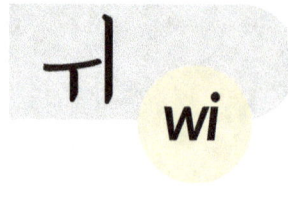

wi

ㅟ is a combination of the vowels ㅜ and ㅣ. To pronounce ㅟ, start by rounding your lips to make the ㅜ sound, like the /oo/ in **Moon.** Then, smoothly transition into the ㅣ sound, similar to the /ee/ in **see** or **week.**

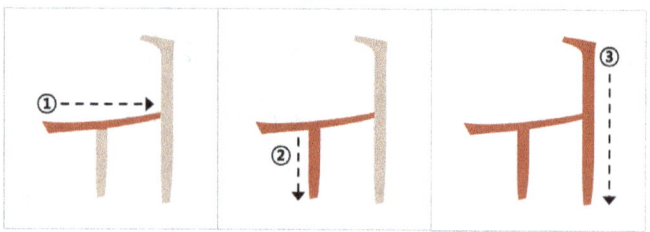

To write ㅟ, start with ㅜ and then add ㅣ to its right.

✏ Follow the correct writing order as you trace ㅟ.

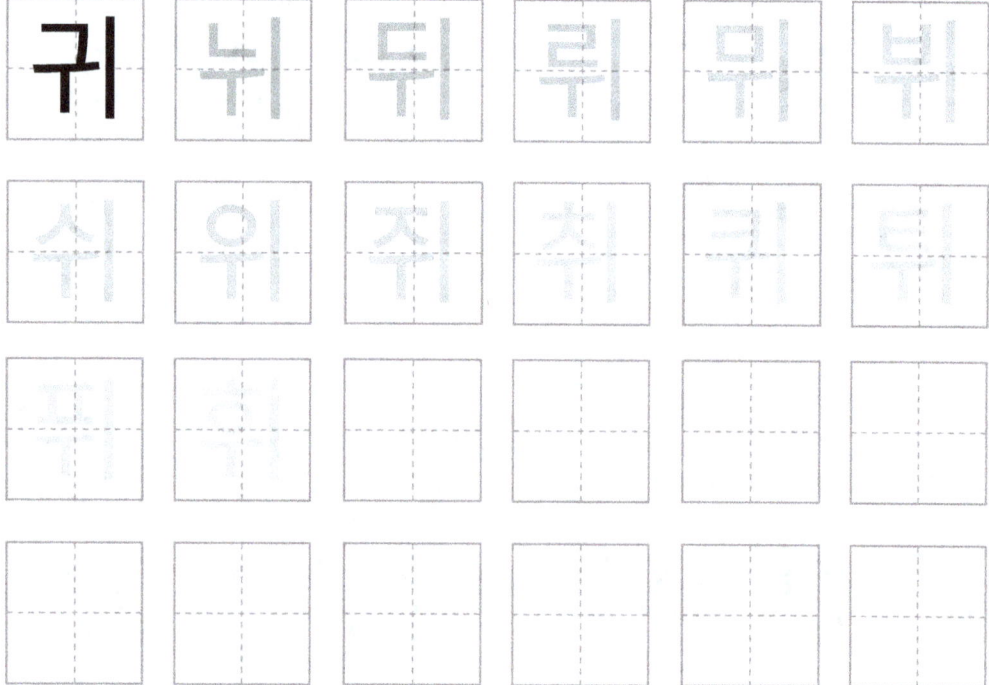

Read the words aloud and trace ㅟ in the syllables.

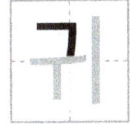

/g<u>wi</u>/
ear

/j<u>wi</u>/
mouse

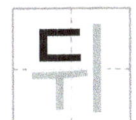

/d<u>wi</u>/
back, behind

/<u>wi</u>/
up, above

/<u>wi</u>—chi/
location, position

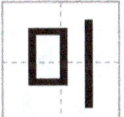

/ch<u>wi</u>—mi/
hobby

DAY
23

ㅢ

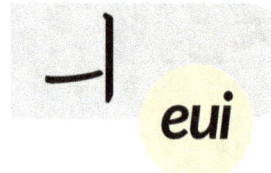

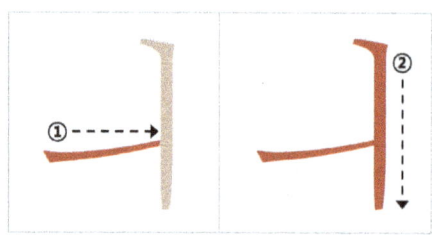

eui

The vowel ㅢ combines ─/eu/ and ㅣ/i/. Start by shaping your mouth for ─/eu/ with lips slightly spread and your tongue flat. Then, move into ㅣ/i/ by raising the front of your tongue. The sound is similar to /eui/ or /ui/.

To write ㅢ, start with ─ and then add ㅣ to its right.

✏ Follow the correct writing order as you trace ㅢ.

Read the words aloud and trace ㅢ in the syllables below.

의 사

/<u>eui</u>−sa/
doctor

의 미

/<u>eui</u>−mi/
meaning, significance

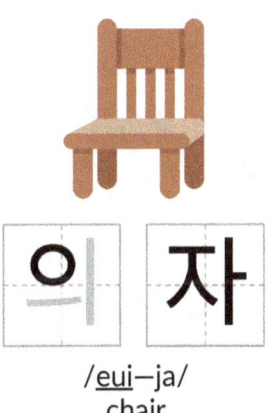

의 자

/<u>eui</u>−ja/
chair

회 의

/hwae−<u>eui</u>/
meeting

히 망

/h<u>eui</u>−mang/
hope

무 늬

/mu−n<u>eui</u>/
pattern

122

Chapter 05

겹받침

DOUBLE FINAL CONSONANTS

DAY 24 Double Final Consonants

11 Double Final Consonants: Function as Batchim ONLY

Double final consonants are pairs of two _different_ consonants that appear together in the 받침 (final consonant) position of a syllable. Their names are easy to understand—you simply read them in the order they appear, starting from the left.

For example:

- The double final ㄺ in 읽다 (*ik—dda, to read*) is called **Rieul—giyok**.
- The double final ㄼ in 밟다 (*bap—dda, to step on*) is called **Rieul—bieup**.

In most cases, when a double final consonant appears at the end of a syllable, **only one of the two is pronounced**. Which consonant remains silent depends on the specific pair. A full table of these rules is provided on the next page.

However, the rule changes when the following syllable begins with a vowel (a syllable starting with the ㅇ). In that case, the normally silent consonant often "carries over" and is pronounced at the start of the next syllable.

In this case:

- The first consonant of the double final consonant is pronounced as the ending sound of the first syllable.
- The second consonant moves to the next syllable and combines with the

vowel to create its sound. Here, the second consonant is pronounced with its basic sound, rather than as its final consonant sound.

- 읽어 (*il–geo*, conjugated form of the verb 읽다) splits into il and geo as the ㄹ(first consonant) and ㄱ(second consonant) are distributed across the two syllables.

Here, ㄱ is pronounced with its basic sound, */g/*, rather than as its final consonant sound, */k/.*

Double final consonants have many exceptions; even native Korean speakers sometimes find them tricky. For instance:

- ㄼ is usually pronounced as ㄹ. However, when the next syllable starts with a vowel, the initial sound of the next syllable is typically ㅂ.
    - 밟다 (*bap–dda, to step on*) and 넓다(*neop–dda, to be broad*) are exceptions where the ㄼ batchim is pronounced as an ㄹ*/l/* sound. But However, some of its derivatives are pronounced with different sounds. In words like 넓죽하다 (*neop–jju–kha–da, to be flat and broad*), 넓둥글다 (*neop–ddung–geul–da, to be broadly rounded*), and 넓데데하다 (*neop–dde–de–ha–da, to be widely spread*), ㄼ sounds as ㅂ*/p/*.

These exceptions are rare, and you'll naturally pick them up as you continue studying Hangul.

HANGUL HACK **The Declining Use of Double Final Consonants**

In modern Korean, the use of double final consonants (겹받침) has steadily declined. For example, In the past, the word for a baby's first

These sound change rules will be explained in more detail with additional examples in Chapter 6.

birthday, 돌/dol/, was written both as 돌/dol/ and 돐/dol/. However, while both forms were used historically, only 돌/dol/ is considered correct today.

Similarly, the final consonant cluster ㄽ was recognized relatively late in the history of Hangul. It was officially included in the *1933 Unified Hangul Orthography* (**한글 맞춤법 통일안**). Despite this recognition, its usage remains very limited and can only be found in a few specific words.

11 Double Final Consonants

	Letter	Pronounciation	Name	When a following syllable starts with a vowel*
When the <u>First</u> Consonant is Pronounced	ㄳ	ㄱ /k/	Giyeok—siot	ㅅ /s/ becomes the next initial sound.
	ㄵ	ㄴ /n/	Nieun—jieut	ㅈ /j/ becomes the next initial sound.
	ㄶ		Nieun—hieut	ㅎ becomes silent.
	ㄼ	ㄹ /l/	Rieul—bieup	ㅂ /b/ becomes the next initial sound.
	ㄽ		Rieul—siot	ㅅ /s/ becomes the next initial sound.
	ㅀ		Rieul—hieut	ㅎ becomes silent.
	ㄾ		Rieul—tieut	⁇ㅌ /s/ becomes the next initial sound.
	ㅄ	ㅂ /p/	Bieup—siot	⁇ㅅ /s/ becomes the next initial sound.
When the <u>Second</u> Consonant is Pronounced	ㄺ	ㄱ /k/	Rieul—giyeok	sounds as ㄹ /l/ + the next initial ㄱ /g/
	ㄿ	ㅍ /p/	Rieul—pieup	sounds as ㄹ /l/ + the next initial ㅍ /p/
	ㄻ	ㅁ /m/	Rieul—mieum	sounds as ㄹ /l/ + the next initial ㅌ /t/

It's not easy to memorize the table of double consonants all at once. However, if you look closely, there's a pattern in how they're pronounced. Here's a simple way to remember it: look at the image on the right and imagine a tiger and a deer. The tiger (the stronger consonant) "overpowers" the deer (the weaker consonant), just like a stronger sound

ㄱ,ㅍ
ㅁ,ㅌ
ㄴ,ㄹ
ㅂ,ㅅ,ㅈ,ㅎ

*Hierarchy of Consonant Strength**

Note: The term "Consonant Strength" is not an official linguistic term. It was created by Miracle Korean as a learning aid to make pronunciation rules easier to understand.

dominates a weaker one. In a double final consonant, <u>the consonant listed higher in the table is the one that gets pronounced.</u> The same rule applies to other combinations. But there's an exception. Some words with ㅄ or ㄼ, like 값 and 넓다, are pronounced using only the ㅂ sound. This is a rare exception within the tier, so keep it in mind as you practice.

Based on the hierarchy of consonant strength, the sound ㄹ is stronger (ranked higher) than ㅂ but weaker (ranked lower) than ㅍ. Keeping this in mind, let's review the table on the previous page. In the syllable ending ㄼ, ㄹ is pronounced, while in ㄿ, ㅍ is pronounced. The same rule applies to other combinations. Try identifying and pronouncing them yourself.

✏️ Practice writing syllables with double final consonants.

삯 삯 삯

/sak/

앉 앉 앉

/an/

앉 /an/

옰 /ol/

않 /an/

값 /gap/

닭 /dak/

읖 /eup/

앎 /am/

핥 /hat/

Read the words aloud and trace each double final consonant in the syllables.

/neo**k**/
soul, spirit, ghost

 다

/a**n**—dda/
to sit

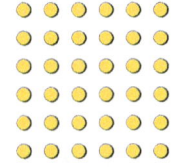

 다

/ma**n**—ta/
to be many, a lot

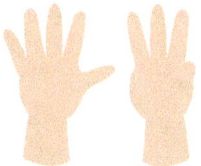

여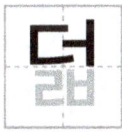

/yeo—deo**l**/
eight

 다

/jja**l**—dda/
to be short

 다

/i**l**—ta/
to lost

/ga<u>p</u>/
price, value

/heu<u>k</u>/
soil, dirt

/sa<u>m</u>/
life

 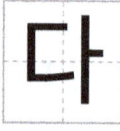

/eu<u>p</u>—dda*/
to recite (a poem, etc.)

/ha<u>l</u>—dda*/
to lick

*읊다 *and* 핥다 *sound different syllable by syllable vs. as whole words—see Chapter 6 for the Sound Change Rules.*

Chapter 06

음운변화
SOUND CHANGE RULES

DAY 25 Sound Change Rules

Why Korean Sounds Different from Its Written Form

Have you ever noticed that Korean sometimes sounds different from how it's written, especially when watching K—dramas or listening to K—pop? This is due to sound change rules.

Sound change rules explain why certain syllables are pronounced differently from how they appear. These shifts depend on the surrounding syllables, helping the language flow more smoothly and naturally. This phenomenon isn't unique to Korean—languages like English and French have similar patterns. Here are a few examples:

- In English, the *r* can change depending on the next word. In **there is /ðɛ:rɪz/**, the *r* is pronounced. But in **there was /ðɛ:wəz/**, the *r* becomes silent to facilitate smooth reading flow.

- In French, there is a rule called **Liaison**: a usually silent consonant at the end of a word is pronounced when the next word begins with a vowel, creating a smooth connection. For example, in **Vous avez**, the *s* is pronounced as **/z/** because **avez** begins with a vowel.

In this chapter, we'll cover six common Korean sound change rules that can help you refine your pronunciation and develop a smoother, more natural flow —closer to that of a native speaker. These rules are usually taught at the intermediate level, so learning them all at once can be tricky. But if you get the basics down early, your listening practice will feel a lot smoother and way less stressful.

Rule 01   Inter–Syllable Sound Shift

Combining Batchim Sound With the Next Vowel—Starting Syllable

Let's quickly review what we learned earlier. Every Korean syllable is made up of at least one consonant and one vowel. When a syllable begins with a vowel, the silent placeholder **ㅇ** is placed in the initial consonant spot. In this case, you only pronounce the vowel sound—no extra consonant sound is added.

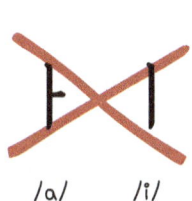

In this section, we'll look at what happens when a syllable with a batchim (final consonant) is followed by a syllable that starts with a vowel. In this case, the final consonant sound 'moves over' and is pronounced at the beginning of the next syllable. This happens because **ㅇ**, when placed at the start of a syllable, is just a silent placeholder—it doesn't add any sound of its own. As a result, the word flows more smoothly and sounds more natural.

Example: 깊어요. (It's deep.)

Let's break this word down:

- The first syllable 깊 has a batchim ㅍ (p sound).
- The next syllable 어요 begins with the vowel ㅓ and the silent ㅇ.

If you read it letter by letter, you might think the pronunciation is */gip—eo—yo/*. However, in natural Korean pronunciation, the **ㅍ** sound *"moves"* to the start of the next syllable, making it: */gi—peo—yo/*.

vowel—starting

깊어요 ⇒ 깊어요 ⇒ 기 어요 ⇒ /기퍼요/

batchim

Try saying both versions out loud:
- */gip—eo—yo/* (reading it separately)
- */gi—peo—yo/* (blending smoothly)

You'll notice that */gi—peo—yo/* flows more naturally, is easier to pronounce, and adjusts the sounds for smoother transitions between syllables.

Rule 02   Sibling Batchim Group*

Some Different Consonants Share the Same Sound

Picture a bunch of ducks swimming in a row. At first glance, they all look similar—almost identical. For someone seeing them for the first time, it might be hard to tell one duck from the other. But of course, each duck is naturally different and unique.

The same idea applies to Korean final consonants. Some consonants look different in writing, just like the ducks, but their sounds are nearly identical when pronounced. These consonants belong to the same 'Sibling Batchim Group'* because they share the same final sound.

Example:

When certain consonants like ㄱ, ㅋ, ㄲ, ㄳ, or ㄺ appear at the end of a syllable, they all take on the same sound as ㄱ/k/.

Note: The term "Sibling Batchim Group" is not an official linguistic term. It was created by Miracle Korean as a learning aid to make pronunciation rules easier to understand.

Why does this happen? In standard Korean pronunciation, the 27 possible final consonants in Hangul are reduced to just seven distinct sounds:

ㄱ, ㄴ, ㄷ, ㄹ, ㅁ, ㅂ, and ㅇ.

This rule applies to even with double consonants.

For example: 막 (*mak*), 맥 (*maek*), and 묶 (*muk*) all end with the ㄱ sound.

Sibling Batchim Groups

	Pronounciation as a Batchim	Sibling Group
Sibling Groups	ㄱ sound	ㄱ, ㅋ, ㄲ, ㄳ, ㄺ
	ㄴ sound	ㄴ
	ㄷ sound	ㄷ, ㅌ, ㅅ, ㅆ, ㅈ, ㅊ, ㄾ, ㄼ
	ㄹ sound	?ㄹ
	ㅁ sound	ㅁ, ㄻ
	ㅂ sound	ㅍ, ㅄ, ㄿ
	ㅇ sound	ㅇ

How Double Batchims Connect to the Following Syllable

When a syllable has a double batchim (two final consonants) and is followed by another syllable, something special happens with the pronunciation. The second consonant of the double batchim connects with the next syllable. What happens next depends on the syllable that follows—whether it _starts with ㅇ or with another consonant_.

Basic Rule

- The first consonant stays in the first syllable as its batchim.
- The second consonant carries over and combines with the vowel in the next syllable.

Think of it like this: the first consonant "stays home," while the second one "moves over" to the next syllable. Keep in mind, this happens no matter what the usual pronunciation rule for that double final consonant might be.

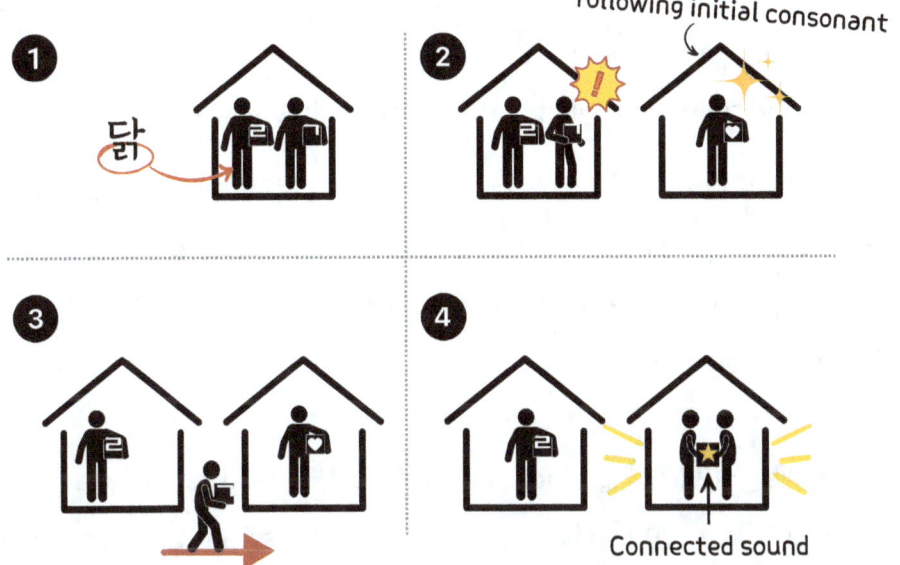

A. When the following syllable begins with ㅇ

The first consonant stays in the first syllable as its batchim. The second consonant moves over and pairs with the vowel in the next syllable. Since ㅇ is silent, the second consonant of the double batchim connects directly with that vowel.

Here's an example:

- 닭 (chicken) is read as /dak/ when it stands alone, following the rule shown in the table on page 128.
- But when a vowel follows, like in 닭이 (chicken + subject marker), the ㄹ sound returns. It's pronounced /dal—gi/.

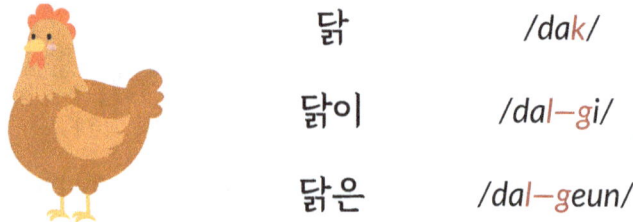

닭	/dak/
닭이	/dal—gi/
닭은	/dal—geun/

B. When the following syllable does not begin with ㅇ

If the syllable following a double final consonant begins with a consonant other than ㅇ, that consonant often changes into an aspirated (breathy) or a tense (stronger) version. As we learned earlier, the tense version of ㄱ is ㄲ, and the aspirated version is ㅋ.

For example, "섞기(mixing)" looks like it should be read as /suk-gi/. However, the second ㄱ in the ㄲ batchim "*pushes*" to the next syllable, strengthening the initial ㄱ. This makes the ㄱ sound tense, so the natural pronunciation becomes /suk-*ggi*/.

Similarly, the word "앉다(to sit)" might look like it should be pronounced /an-*da*/. But the ㅈ from the ㄵ batchim combines with the following ㄷ, causing ㄷ to become tense. As a result, the natural pronunciation is /an-*dda*/.

Finally, for comparison, take the word 핥다 (to lick). On its own, it's usually pronounced /hat-da/. But in 핥으니 (to lick + marker), the double batchim ㄹㅌ splits apart. The ㄹ sound stays in the first syllable, giving hal—, while the ㅌ sound moves over to the next vowel, making *teu—ni*. Put together, the word is pronounced /hal-teu-ni/.

C. Exception: ㄼ and ㅄ

According to the exception on page 128, when ㄼ or ㅄ appear as a batchim, only the ㅂ sound is pronounced. However, if the following syllable begins with ㅇ, the ㄹ sound comes back. On the other hand, if the following syllable starts with a consonant, only the consonant sound strengthens into its tense version.

- Examples where the next syllable starts with ㅇ:
    - 밟아요 (steps on) → /bap-a-yo/ (x) → /bal-ba-yo/ (O)
    - 넓은 (wide, adj. form) → /neop-eun/ (x) → /neol-beun/ (O)

- Examples where the next syllable starts with a consonant:
    - 밟다 (to step on) → /bap-da/ (x) → /bap-dda/ (O)
    - 넓다 (wide) → /neop-da/ (x) → /neop-dda/ (O)

Rule 03 Sound Shift in Batchim ㅎ

The Batchim ㅎ Becomes Silent When Followed by ㅇ

Rule II applies in other cases, with one key exception: when ㅎ appears as a final consonant (batchim), either alone or as part of ㄶ or ㅀ, it is not pronounced if the following syllable begins with a vowel. For example:

- 좋아요. (I like it.)
- Pronunciation: 조아요 /jo–a–yo/ (not: /joh–a–yo/ or /jo–ha–yo/)

When the final consonant ㅎ is followed by ㅇ in the next syllable, its sound disappears completely, resulting in a smooth pronunciation flow. Imagine the batchim ㅎ as a small spark and a vowel–only syllable as water; when they combine, they neutralize each other.

vowel–only

좋아요 ⇒ 좋아요 ⇒ 조 아요 ⇒ /조아요/

ㅎ
(final consonant)

The Batchim ㅎ Strengthens ㄱ, ㄷ, ㅅ, and ㅈ

However, don't underestimate the batchim ㅎ just because its sound vanishes in this context. As a final consonant, ㅎ is far from weak—it sometimes acts as a catalyst, intensifying the pronunciation of certain initial consonants in the following syllable. Specifically, when the batchim ㅎ is followed by a syllable starting with ㄱ, ㄷ, ㅅ, or ㅈ, these consonants change to their aspirated (ㅋ, ㅌ, ㅊ) or tense (ㅆ) forms. The reason only ㅅ becomes tense in this case is because ㅅ doesn't have an aspirated counterpart.

ㅎ
(final consonant) ㄱ,ㄷ,ㅅ,ㅈ ㅋ,ㅌ,ㅆ,ㅊ

Examples of Sound Shift in Batchim ㅎ

Word (ㅎ+Consonant)	Meaning	Pronunciation
싫고 (ㄱ→ㅋ)	unsatisfying; disagreeable	/sil–ko/
하찮다 (ㄷ → ㅌ)	to be minor, clumsy	/ha–chan–ta/
많습니다 (ㅅ → ㅆ)	to exist in abundance	/man–sseum–ni–da/
끓지 (ㅈ → ㅊ)	boiling	/kkeul–chi/

HANGUL HACK **Tip for Remembering**

This rule might feel tricky, but here is a simple phrase to help you memorize it: *Good Dogs Sit and Jump Happily!*

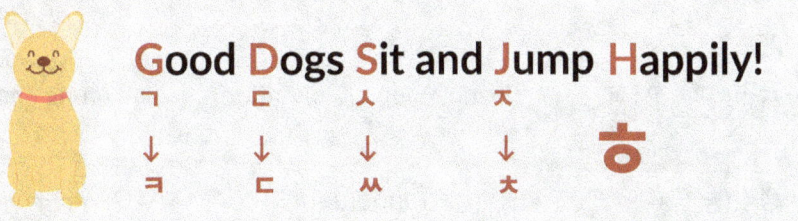

Good **D**ogs **S**it and **J**ump **H**appily!

ㄱ   ㄷ   ㅅ   ㅈ

↓   ↓   ↓   ↓   ㅎ

ㅋ   ㄷ   ㅆ   ㅊ

Rule 04   Nasal Assimilation

Sounds Near Nasal Sounds Become ?Nasalized

Nasal sounds in Hangul are made when air flows through the nose. These sounds include ㄴ, ㅁ, and ㅇ. Nasal assimilation happens when certain consonants—like ㅂ, ㄱ, and ㄹ—change to sound more like nasal sounds when they come directly before or after one.

For example:

- When ㅂ appears before a nasal sound, it changes to ㅁ.
- When ㄱ appears before a nasal sound, it changes to ㅇ.
- When ㄹ follows a nasal sound, it changes to ㄴ for smoother pronunciation.

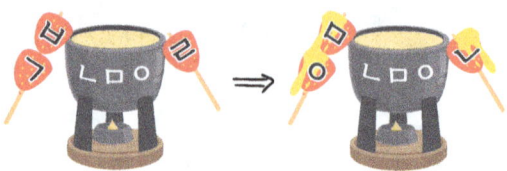

These transformations allow sounds to connect more easily, making pronunciation feel effortless and fluid. Take a look at the examples below.

Example	Meaning	Pronunciation
밥물(ㅂ→ㅁ)	cooking water for rice	/bam—mul/
국민(ㄱ → ㅇ)	citizen, people of a nation	/gung—min/
정리(ㄹ → ㄴ)	arrangement	/jung—ni/

Rule 05 Lateralization

ㄴ changes to a ㄹ sound when it comes before or after ㄹ

When ㄴ appears right before or right after ㄹ in a word, its pronunciation changes to ㄹ. This process is called **유음화** (*Yueumhwa*), or *Lateralization*, in Korean.

Why does this happen? The ㄹ sound is a lateral consonant, which means it allows air to flow smoothly around the tongue with minimal obstruction—similar to the English /l/ sound. Because of this, it feels more natural for ㄴ to shift to ㄹ when they are next to each other. Take a look at the examples below.

Word	Meaning	Pronunciation
난로 (ㄴ→ㄹ)	heater	/nal—lo/ (not /nan—ro/)
신라 (ㄴ→ㄹ)	an ancient Korean kingdom that existed between 57 BCE – 935CE	/sil—la/ (not /sin—ra/)
줄넘기 (ㄴ→ㄹ)	jump rope	/jul—lum—ggi/ (not jul—num—ggi/)

I'm actually a ㄴ

ㄹ

ㄹ

ㄹ

Exception: When ㄹ Becomes a ㄴ Sound

There are some exceptions where ㄹ is pronounced as ㄴ, especially in certain compound words that use Sino—Korean characters (borrowed from Chinese). For example, when syllables like 란, 량, 력, 레, 로, 료, or 류 appear in specific compound words, the usual ㄹ sound (like /l/ or /r/) changes to ㄴ /n/. For now, you don't need to memorize this rule yet! These exceptions are a bit more advanced, and they're not terms you'll use very often. So think of this as a helpful extra note for later on. Here are some examples:

Examples of When ㄹ Becomes a ㄴ Sound

Example	Meaning	Sino—letter	Pronunciation
의견란	comment section	欄(란)	/eui—gyeon—nan/
생산량	production volume	量(량)	/saeng—san—nyang/
결단력	decisiveness	力(력)	/gyeol—ddan—nyeok/
공권력	government, authority	力(력)	/gong—ggwon—nyeok/
상견례	first meeting	禮(례)	/sang—gyeon—nye/
횡단로	crosswalk	路(로)	/hoeng—dan—no/
입원료	hospitalization fee	料(료)	/i—bwon—nyo/

Rule 06 Palatalization

ㄷ and ㅌ Change to ㅈ and ㅊ Sounds

In English, when you say *"and you"*, the pronunciation often blends into /æn–dʒu/ or /ən–ju/ instead of the more rigid /æn–du/. This shift makes the words flow more smoothly. Korean has a similar concept called **Palatalization**.

Palatal sounds, like ㅈ and ㅊ, are made by the tongue touching the highest part of the mouth. Palatalization happens when the final consonants ㄷ/d/ or ㅌ/t/ appear before a vowel that begins with a y–sound (like ㅠ, ㅛ, ㅕ, or ㅑ) or the vowels 이/i/, 히/hi/. When this happens:

A. ㄷ/d/ → ㅈ/j/

- The consonant ㄷ/d/ changes to ㅈ/j/ when it's followed by the vowel 이/i./
- Example: 굳이 /gud–i/ → pronounced 구지 /gu–ji/

B. ㅌ/t/ → ㅊ/ch/

- The consonant ㅌ/t/ changes to ㅊ/ch/ when it's followed by the vowel 이/i./
- Example: 같이/gat–i/ → pronounced 가치/ga–chi/

This palatalization is called **구개음화 (gu–gae–eum–hwa)** in Korean. In this term, **화** means to become. Through palatalization, non–palatal sounds like ㄷ and ㅌ shift to palatal sounds ㅈ and ㅊ. This change happens because your tongue naturally moves closer to the roof of your mouth, making the sound easier and more natural to pronounce.

The table below shows examples of palatalization.

Examples of Palatalization

Example	Meaning	Pronunciation
같이	together	/ga–chi/
굳이	deliberately, insistently	/gu–ji/
붙여	attaching, putting together	/bu–chyeo/
해돋이	sunrise	/hae–do–ji/
미닫이	sliding door	/mi–da–ji/
묻히다	to be buried	/mu–chi–da/
밑이	bottom	/mi–chi/

Reading Practice

📖 Read the sentences aloud applying the six sound change rules.

1. 나는 밥을 먹는다.

Meaning	I am eating rice.
Pronunciation	/na–neun ba–beul meong–neun–da/
Explanation	**밥을** According to Rule 1, when a word ends with batchim like ㅂ and is followed by a particle like 을, the pronunciation often inserts a short vowel sound to make it easier to say. Therefore, **밥을** is pronounced /ba–beul/ instead of /bab–eul/.
	먹는다 According to Rule 4, when a word has a batchim ㄱ (the final sound of **먹**) followed by the syllable 는, the ㄱ sound changes to ㅇ (ng sound). This creates a smoother flow in pronunciation. As a result, **먹는다** is pronounced /meong–neun–da/ instead of /meok–neun–da/.

2. 나는 나비를 잡는다.

Meaning	I am catching a butterfly.
Pronunciation	/na—neun na—bi—reul jam—neun—da/
Explanation 잡는다	In **잡는다**, according to Rule 4, the batchim ㅂ before the second syllable 는 changes to the ㅇ sound. As a result, **잡는다** is pronounced as /jam—neun—da./

3. 공부는 끝이 없다.

Meaning	There's no end to studying.
Pronunciation	/gong—bu—neun kkeu—chi eop—dda/
Explanation 끝이	In **끝이**, because the syllable 이 follows the ㅌ batchim (final consonant) in the previous syllable, Rule 6 causes ㅌ to be pronounced as ㅊ. Then, according to Rule 1, this ㅊ combines smoothly with the vowel in the following syllable. As a result, **끝이** is pronounced as /kkeu—chi/.
없다	In **없다**, Rule 2 applies: the double final consonant in the first syllable is split for pronunciation. However, since two consonants cannot occur together in the initial position of a syllable, the ㄷ is pronounced with slightly stronger emphasis, naturally indicating the presence of the combined consonants.

4. 생산량이 늘어나요.

Meaning	The production volume is increasing.
Pronunciation	/saeng—san—nyang—i neu—reo—na—yo/

Explanation		
	생산량이	According to Rule 5, **산** is positioned before **량**, so it would typically be pronounced as **/살량/**. However, because **량** is a Sino—Korean character that carries an independent meaning, it is considered an exception. As a result, the **ㄹ** sound changes to an **ㄴ** sound, and the word is pronounced as */saeng—san—nyang/*.
	늘어나요	늘어나요 follows Rule 1 and is pronounced as */neu—reo—na—yo/*.

5. 박물관이 좋아요.

Meaning	I like the museum.
Pronunciation	/bang—mul—gwa—ni jo—a—yo/

Explanation		
	박물관이	According to Rule 4, the **박** sound in the first syllable changes to **/방/** due to the influence of the initial consonant **ㅁ** in the second syllable **물**. As a result, **박물관** is pronounced */bang—mul—gwan/*, rather than */bak—mul—gwan/*.
	좋아요	In **좋아요**, the **ㅎ** in **좋** becomes silent when followed by **ㅇ** in **아**, as explained by Rule 3.

축하합니다! You are now a Hangul master, and we hope this journey has brought you lots of fun and excitement.

Miracle Korean exists because of readers like you, who are passionate about learning Korean. To show our gratitude, we are committed to supporting you throughout your language journey by consistently providing practical and effective learning materials. We aim to develop more resources that reflect real—life Korean usage, ensuring you gain skills applicable in everyday situations. We look forward to continuing this journey together and celebrating your progress along the way.

In the next book, we will take a closer look at useful Korean expressions and grammar. You will also learn tips to help you speak and use Korean even more naturally. We are so proud of how far you have come, and we can't wait to see where this journey takes you next. Until then, take care, and keep practicing. See you soon! ੭(*´꒳`*)੭

With warm wishes,

오리도리

www.ingramcontent.com/pod-product-compliance
Lightning Source LLC
Chambersburg PA
CBHW081535120626

46550CB00009B/2736